Praise for Mary Lyons and her Wisdom Lessons

At Standing Rock Mary Lyons shared her knowledge and lifted people's spirits. Grandma Mary is a big-hearted and generous teacher, who won't always tell you what you want to hear. But it's usually the advice and counsel you need to hear.

— Journalist and filmmaker Leana Hosea

Grandmother Mary Lyons is a true Wisdom Keeper. Each chapter of this wonderful book is a gift! Grandmother Mary's loving presence in our lives is an example of her truth as she lives and breathes the breaths of her ancestors. In each moment you spend with her you know you are in the presence of an elder who has walked the path of life true to the sacred teachings of Mother Earth.

— Patricia Morris Cardona, APRN, BC, and Daniel J. Cardona, MD, co-founders of The Cosmic Mysteries School

When I first met Grandmother Mary at the Omega Institute in the fall of 2016 I was truly touched by her wisdom, her beautiful sense of humor and her incredible spirit. I have also had the pleasure of hosting her and two other grandmothers in Chicago, where she continued to inspire others with her stories and through her love.

— Tony Hollenback, LCSW, Director of Family Services, Niles, Illinois

I knew of Great Grandma Lyons long before I met her. I was in awe of her aura of deep spiritual calling and her natural leadership. Mary Lyons is a reminder that our spirit lies within our character and that is the strength of our Indigenous culture.

— Mary Kunesh-Podein, Minnesota State Representative

It has become part of my Spiritual Practice to read one of Great Grandmother Mary Lyons' Wisdom Lessons online in the morning and then lean into to each lesson as I move through my day. What a gift to have all of these wise words and more compiled into one book. This is a book that will empower generations. We need to listen NOW to the voices of our Elders while we still have them with us. Mary Lyon's voice needs to be heard in this pivotal time of upheaval and change.

— Holley Rauen, RN Midwife, Co-founder,
Pachamama Alliance of SW Florida

It is a great pleasure and privilege to provide some words of *aroha* (love) and *manaaki* (support) for Great Grandmother Mary Lyons. I have come to know her love for Indigenous people over the years, through her connection with us here in Aotearoa/New Zealand. We treasure Mary's words of wisdom, and are in awe of her brave stand in the face of adversity, as well as her tireless fight for the freedom of Indigenous people all over the world. *Nga mihi aroha* Mary.

— Ngaroimata Reid, President, Te Atatu Branch,
Te Ropu Wahine Maori toko i te Ora
(Maori Women's Welfare League),
Aotearoa/New Zealand

As a Traditional Maori Wisdom Keeper, who has represented New Zealand internationally and interacted with more than 150 Nations, I have had the pleasure and honor of sharing traditional and cultural knowledge with Great-grandmother Mary Lyons at an International Conference of Religions at Salt Lake City in the USA, as well as traditional Maori gatherings in New Zealand. Both of us believe in being One with the whole of Creation, and identify with both Papatuanuku/Earth Mother, and Ranginui/Sky Father. Through the Wisdom Lessons shared by Great- grandmother Mary Lyons, people will be able to appreciate the tremendous guidance and insight of an Indigenous Great-grandmother who can speak with authority, because her knowledge comes from first-hand experience. Great-grandmother Mary Lyons stands up with great pride, through the vested authority that she has from her ancestors and the Creator.

— Dr. Rosemarie Lambert Rangimarie Pere, CM, CBE

Grandmother Mary's words always inspire and uplift me. She makes me feel all is and will be right with the world. Thank you Grandmother Mary Lyons.

— Sharon Ziegler

A woman who carries knowledge with a genuine smile— this is how Mary provides healing & love for her people.

— Paula Looking Horse

Mary's leadership and indigenous lessons are the hope for a world in which the majority of people have lost their way, disconnected from nature, themselves and one another. We need to be connected to Source, to Mother Earth, to Creator, to the Divine Feminine and Masculine. Mary's lessons will help us heal from the brokenness and to be empowered to become the spiritual leaders needed now. Her teachings that we are nature and how to live in harmony with nature are the most important lessons to transform the violence and learn the ancient ways of how to care for creation.

— Ann L. Smith, Director of Circle Connections, Convener of the Millionth Circle, and Regional Coordinator of Gather The Women

I wish to express my deep regard for Grandmother Mary Lyons. There are many parallel experiences between our First Nations people that enable the communities to share knowledge and experience to their global brothers and sisters. Grandmother Mary Lyons plays a significant role in connecting us all globally, sharing knowledge and providing spiritual guidance that will give us all strength to maintain, respect and celebrate culture.

— Belinda Mason, Creative Director, Blur Projects, Australia

Endorsing the wisdom of the grandmothers, connecting us from high mountains and across deep oceans, ever guiding, ever teaching, ever showing us the way.

— Pua Case Kanaka Maoli, Mauna Kea 'Ohana, Hawai'i

I am honored to say that Mary and I have been sister friends for over twenty years. Mary is kind, gentle, determined and soulful. She teaches us the importance of connection, love, compassion and respect for people and our land. Her wisdom has changed my life.

— Ginny Blade, Program Manager, Adoption Support Network, NACAC, St. Paul, Minnesota

When I am an elder, I hope to have half the wisdom and sacred knowledge that Grandmother Mary has. Her book is a testament to the strength of our ancestors and the hope of the future. She reminds me how strong I am and that every day is a new day. Her book inspires me to remember the past and look towards the future, all while living and laughing in the moment.

— Kathryn Holt Richardson, J.D.

We are very proud and inspired by Great Grandmother Mary Lyons. She brings the voice of many communities' concerns to the forefront and shares positive healing energy.

— Doreen Bennett, New Zealand

WISDOM LESSONS

Cover photo montage and front cover
author photo by Jane Feldman

Back cover author photo by Martina Thalhofer

Cover and page design by Anna Myers Sabatini

Library of Congress Control Number: 2018954574
ISBN: 978-0-9861980-9-0

Lyons, Mary, 1953-
Wisdom lessons : spirited guidance from an Ojibwe
great-grandmother / by Mary Lyons; edited by
Jennifer Browdy and Grace Rossman.
Housatonic, Massachusetts : Green Fire Press, [2018], ©2018.
xx, 223 pages : illustrations ; 21 cm
9780986198090
1. Lyons, Mary, 1953- 2. Spiritual life. 3. Ojibwa Indians -
Religion. 4. Ojibwa Indians - Biography.
I. 7001 Browdy, Jennifer. II. Rossman, Grace.
E99.C6 L96 2018 | 299.7/8333 (23 ed.)

Green
Fire
Press

Green Fire Press
PO Box 377 Housatonic MA 01236

WISDOM LESSONS

Spirited Guidance
from an Ojibwe Great-Grandmother

By Mary Lyons

Edited by Jennifer Browdy and Grace Rossman

Green Fire Press

Housatonic
Massachusetts

Dedication

To my elders, grandparents and parents: Life was so much richer thanks to the teachings that you gifted and entrusted me to carry and move forward.

To Jennifer Browdy: I would not have had the ambition to move forward with this book if it were not for your belief and motivation to put this together. I will be forever grateful for your long hours of hard work as you directed the process of making this happen. Not only are you my publisher, you have become a sister whom I treasure during this lifetime.

To Grace Rossman: thank you for your belief in this book as well, and for your help in assisting Jennifer and compiling such beautiful promotional materials for the book. It's an honor for me to have a young person like you embracing the messages of these Wisdom Lessons, and I will hold this dear forever.

To all the individuals out there who thought they did not count in this life, you all were my courage and strength to sing the words of our ancestors: "We Matter."

To my family and friends; you all know who you are. Thank you for your patience and understanding, and most of all for your encouragement and belief in this journey.

Blessing the waters. Photo by Jane Feldman

Prayer of Choice

May I close my eyes,
feel my spirit soar
and know that I will make my relatives proud
of the choices I make today.

WISDOM LESSONS

My mother Catherine "Ruby" White-Lyons, in a picture taken in the early 1950's. This was our house in Bena, Minnesota. Just about every other day she did the laundry by scrub board or an old hand washer and would hang the clothes out to dry rain or shine, whether it was snowing or, as she used to say, a "heat wave." She was always in a house coat when she was home.

Prologue

FOLLOWING THE PATH OF THE ANCESTORS

Ancestral history

My native name is Nish-Nibi-Ikwe, meaning Second Water Woman. My English given name is Mary Lyons. My father told the story of how we received our English names through the United States Government Bureau of Indian Affairs, as they could not pronounce our original native names. His father told him that a French soldier from Lyon, France gave the name of "Lyon" to many within our tribes. When we were processed into the Reservation systems, the families with this name became the "Lyons." Today, many are legally changing their given family names back to their original native names.

I come from a family of fifteen—my mother, my father and thirteen of us children. I am from the part of Minnesota where the invisible line stretches between Canada and the United States. Many Ojibwe people settled here, having relocated from the East Coast hundreds of years ago.

My knowledge of the Ojibwe tribe comes from a link that stretches back to the early 1700s, spanning four generations of storytelling. My father, Charles Frederick Lyons Sr., who went by "Charlie," was born in 1889. We never corrected his tombstone, which says he was born in 1890. According to my father's memory and what is recorded in the Bureau of Indian Affairs Registry, his mother, my paternal grandmother, was born in 1836. Her mother, my great-grandmother, was born in 1784 and was 52 when she gave birth to my grandmother.

My grandfather on my mother's side was born in the late 1800s, and his mother was born in the mid 1800s. My grandfather was John Jacob White, an Ojibwe elder from the Leech Lake Reservation in Northern Minnesota, in the Onigum and Sugar Point area. He was a child during the last Indian War in Minnesota. My maternal grandmother's English given name was Lillian West. I always loved her name, as it sounded to me like a novel waiting to be written; I imagined she must have had an exciting life.

Sadly, my mother, Catherine "Ruby" White-Lyons, told a different story of my grandmother. My mother told us that she was a small woman with a quiet voice, a hard worker who got sick often; she may have had diabetes. After years of struggling with her health, my maternal grandmother passed away and my grandfather remarried.

Early years: life on the reservation

I grew up on the Leech Lake Reservation in the small township of Bena, Minnesota. Growing up on a reservation in the mid-1900s had its ups and downs. When we were little, we had no electricity, running water, or indoor bathrooms. We had cellars for refrigeration, dirt floors for air conditioning in the summer, and outdoor composting bathrooms. Our heating system in the winter was a wood stove that stood in the center of our two-room home, and our insulation was shoveled dirt covered by tar paper. Our food supply came from the gifts of Mother Nature: berries, potatoes, fish, deer, and our beautiful wild rice, which grew above the waters that had originally drawn our people to the territories of northern Minnesota.

Our summer playground was nature. Our libraries were the elders, who told us stories during the cold winters. We were blessed with unconditional love, not just from humans, but also from our animal relatives of the water and forest. All the elements sang to us as long as we honored them.

As children, we had limited contact with the outside world. We did not know that there was a world out there that was full of prejudice against the original people. My family experienced the government removal of children and the displacement of our family values. This was a painful time for me and my entire family.

During my early years, I witnessed a happy life turn to a destructive life. Alcohol made a big appearance in our town and within our family. I witnessed personality changes in the children in my community, and I sensed that something was wrong, but I just couldn't put a finger on it. Later in life, I realized it was fetal alcohol syndrome, and the strange, difficult behaviors I saw in children around me were their disabilities.

I would witness anger within a family that I had known to be a loving family. I would go home and ask my father why they acted this way. He would always correct me about judging others and remind me that there was a lesson in what I was seeing; in a caring way, he would always bring me back to balance.

During these times, we didn't know from day to day if the children we played with would be there in the morning, as the welfare system was taking children like crazy. My family did not escape from this. Whatever had happened to my mother in boarding school haunted her and she just couldn't seem to get life right; she was a drinker. On the days when she was sober at home, which were rare, she would be great with my brothers, but she was really hard on my sisters and me. Sometimes it felt like she didn't like us because we were girls. My father always compensated for her behavior. He would remind us not to judge others, and not to pity ourselves.

A year before she died, my mother had moved from the reservation to the city with the youngest children. During that time, she started to clean herself up and was thinking about coming home; she seemed happy. In her final year of life, she lived with the aim of getting everything right, starting with moving home with the two youngest children. Her commitment to being a good mom and wife was there, she just needed to get back home to the reservation.

My father knew she was with child and was extremely excited at all the hard work she had done, caring for her health and wellness. She had promised him she would never again leave him and us. Several days before she was to return home with the two youngest children, she got sick, fell asleep and never woke up again. My mother passed away at the age of 43, in a diabetic coma. The story goes that a family friend came over to visit, and my youngest sister answered the door. She told the family friend that our mother had been sleeping for a long time and that her body was cold. This experience was something my younger sister could never forget throughout her lifetime. My mother died when I was eleven, and on the day she was buried I felt happy because I knew she was no longer hurting. I felt comfort knowing that I would always know where she was, and that I could visit her everyday and she would not yell at me. She would listen to me; she could not ignore me. I knew she had turned into an angel, and I thought angels were nice.

After my mother passed, my father remained on the reservation in northern Minnesota. He was a strong man and our native community loved and respected him highly. He and his older brother Bill Lyons owned a small fishing company called Lyons Landing on Lake Winnibigoshish, Minnesota. He continued to raise

My father, 'Charlie Lyons," in a picture from the early 1950s. There was never a day off for him; he would often say that his father would tell him, 'You will have plenty of time to rest when you return home to the Grand Circle of Life.'

the younger children until the welfare came for the two youngest as they thought he was too old to care for them. They were placed in foster care and then the government continued to try to adopt them out. They said they were monitoring my mother's children closely because she had already lost a child to adoption, due to abandonment.

These were dark times that are very difficult to talk about; I keep these memories in the resting place of my mind. These experiences are what led me to my work of finding the missing children of the foster care system. I still have a brother by the name of Randall Lyons out there; we never found him again after he was taken from our family and put up for adoption. I am always searching and hoping to find him, just to let him know that we have never forgotten him, that he is loved. This history always gets the tears flowing as my thoughts awaken.

Life growing up had its challenges. We witnessed the dismantling of our families as a result of the Indian Removal Acts, which gave the government the right to take Indian childen from their families and put them into the hands of boarding schools, orphanages, foster homes and adoption agencies. Even though the pain was great, we took courage from our ancestors' stories of the challenges they faced and overcame. We were taught never to pity ourselves, and to view our own struggles as this world's lessons. We were taught to pity and pray for the people we found challenging, as they did not know the real value of life and the meaning of unconditional love.

Coming into adulthood

Life went on, and I grew up. I married at 18 and had two daughters. In the early 1970s, I was restless in my marriage, and starting to venture into the world of drinking. My mother-in-law, who always felt like a mother to me, was helpful to me during this time. She told me, "I don't know what's going on with you, but you need to go and get it out of your system. When you are ready to come home, your daughters will be here for you."

I felt the need to adventure on Mother Earth, so I left the Native American communities and stepped into an unknown world. I traveled throughout the United States, Canada, England, Germany, India and Mexico on my own, experiencing life to the fullest. I worked odd jobs, from teaching to sales. Fortunately, I was accepted in the white world and learned sales very quickly. I began to make the money I always knew I could. During this time, I was drinking what I thought was "socially," and I would also occasionally do drugs. Eventually I became dependent on heroin.

One day, after I had been addicted for nearly a decade, my mother-in-law called me and said, "You need to be done with whatever you're doing and come home and take care of these girls." I did just that, although it took me several rounds of treatment in different rehab centers to get well. I finally took my life back and I came home after being absent from my daughters for ten years. They didn't know me—they only knew of me.

Returning home was the most difficult time of my life, as I had to admit to myself that I was trying to understand my mother by living as I thought she had lived.

My life began again after returning home. All my ancestral knowledge began to awaken within me. My spirit woke up from all the smothering I had inflicted on myself. During this time, I started having recurring dreams, and the messages were always the same: you can't teach something unless you have experienced the journey that Creator laid out for you.

Following the path of the ancestors

Life began to blossom for me, as Creator put mountains before me that only he/she knew I could climb. In addition to my two girls, I have seven sons, three of whom are my little sister Cathy's children—she was murdered in 1989 on New Year's Eve. This tragedy helped pave a pathway for me to the forgotten Indigenous women, transgender and LGBT communities, as so many go missing and murdered without a thought. These young people taught me a lot; I saw in them many of my own mistakes, which I had learned from my mother. It wasn't until later that I fully understood the real meaning of mirror teachings and knew this had to change or we would be repeating another cycle of disparities and pain.

My grandfather and father always told me that just when I thought I knew everything, Creator would remind me that I promised I would always walk as a student and a difficult lesson would appear on my path. My children now have their own families and all have their ups and downs. I have to be reminded that each journey they take is theirs and I cannot try to fix it. All I can do is be a great listener and give them patterns of life's lessons to help them understand their own journeys.

I have been working in the child welfare field for some 35 years now, and spending my spare time helping others through recovery; this became my full-time volunteer work. I am honored to be part of a group of foster parents that started the first foster care agency in Minnesota, more than thirty years ago. This same group started Minnesota Coalition of Fetal Alcohol Syndrome Disorder (FASD), and created another agency dedicated to raising awareness about issues related to FASD. This agency later turned into one of the biggest information-based non-profit agencies in the Midwest.

During my time at the adoption support agency, another colleague and I created an organization called Celebrating the Native Child. The organization offered conferences led exclusively by Native professionals for Native children who were adopted or in foster homes, or who were trying to find their families.

I was honored to work with an adult adoptee who had returned home, along with a spiritual elder man in ceremonies that honored the returned children. The spiritual elder has passed away, but the adult returnee has helped the project blossom into an annual event.

Minnesota Senator Norm Coleman nominated me for a Congressional Award called "Angels In Adoption," which was awarded to me in Washington DC in 2006. This award means a lot to me, as it is a reminder to me about my own growth, change, and learning.

Over many years, I have had the pleasure of fostering hundreds of children. During this time, I made

My dear sisters from Women of Wellbriety International (WOWI). Linda Woods is from Michigan and sits on the Four Grandmothers Council, as I do as well. Sharyl Bloom WhiteHawk is the founder of WOWI. These women keep this organization alive and helpful to all who need support to live clean and sober. These two ladies are very special to me as they are my strength when I am feeling low. WOWI is a 100% volunteer organization.

mistakes and learned from professionals to correct my faults and to improve my parenting of special needs children. Throughout my journey, I have learned how to correct myself by remembering who I really am.

I always knew there would be blessings in my life and that the rewards would come from the awakening spirits of many that I would meet along life's path. I knew that it would be important to share the lessons of wisdom that had been passed down, to help others see the light to a brighter life. Once I accepted this pathway, the ancestral knowledge just flowed and blossomed.

At a very early age, I helped many of our community elders and listened very closely to the guidance they offered from our traditions. I always knew I would continue on the pathway they laid out for me, but I fought it for a while, in my early years. It wasn't until my 40's that I chose to surrender to the journey and trust in Creator to guide me.

During my 40's and early 50's I went through intense training with the elders; as soon as one would leave this world and their space here on earth came available, one of us younger ones would be called to serve in their place. It was not like there were any formal dinners or appointments or legal papers; the people would just start coming to you for guidance and help. The world would start seeking you out, trusting and believing in you, and you just had to be present with your full will to receive the guidance offered by Creator.

More recently I have been traveling again, throughout the United States as well as internationally. I spend two weeks in April at the United Nations in New York City, at the UN Forum on Indigenous Issues, which deals with topics ranging from caring for the Earth and water, to missing and murdered women and everything else in between. I have traveled to New Zealand with the Grandmothers of the Sacred WE, receiving direction and guidance from our Maori eldest grandmother, Rose Pere. I have also been invited to attend a gathering of indigenous elders in Greenland, learning from my brother Angaangagaaqa, an Inuit elder who is the keeper of his tribal wisdom and especially wise when it comes to water issues.

The Wisdom Lessons are for everyone

The Wisdom Lessons in this book come from my whole life experience, including all the wise elders I have learned from and worked with. These teachings are for anyone who feels stuck and is looking for help in understanding life, as well as support in moving forward. I believe these teachings will be of benefit to people of any age and any background, from a young child to the eldest person on the planet, no matter the color of their skin or their religion or culture.

In sharing these Wisdom Lessons with the world, I hope to help create happier communities, especially among those people who thought they were useless and didn't count. I hope that when they see that they matter, as we all do, they will become stronger and more content.

Photo by Martina Thalhofer

I. DANCING WITH THE ANCESTORS

If We Do Not Listen

There was a time when babies were born healthy,

There was a time when children played with laughter,

There was a time when young people expressed themselves,

There was a time when we witnessed our generations coming to Eldership.

Yesterday, our babies were born into loving families with both parents,

Yesterday, our young children ran happily through our communities without fear,

Yesterday, our young people were listened to,

Yesterday, our circles were full—with children, young adults, parents, grandparents and great-grandparents.

Today, our babies are struggling for life,

Today, our children are scattered,

Today, our young people are vanishing,

Today, our family system is in a state of chaos.

Tomorrow is not promised to a baby

If we do not teach the traditional practices of
nurturing.

Tomorrow is not promised to a child

If we do not take care of ourselves and become
healthy parents.

Tomorrow is not promised to a young person

If we do not help change this society for their benefit.

Tomorrow is not promised to an elder

If we do not start healing our communities and caring
for the ones who raised us.

If we do not listen to ourselves, our ancestors will
vanish and we will be no more.

Sending tobacco prayers out to all to remind them to
awaken their spirits and care for themselves. Life was
blessed in the old days, when family was family and
our lives were alcohol- and drug-free.

Little Spirits

The Grandmother Circle presents these Little Spirits,

These little ones who are sent to Mother Earth with
a mission.

Mothers who are gifted these Little Spirits are chosen,

The lessons these little ones are about to teach are
lessons that have been forgotten.

The gifts these Little Spirits offer are for all to share;

We all get to share in unwrapping the joy

Of their journey through this life.

When you encounter these little ones, welcome
their lessons.

We often think we are the teachers to these Little
Spirits.

At one time, we may have been, until many of us
entered dark alleys of life.

Then, they became our teachers, the light at the end
of these dark places.

Be gentle, be patient, be loving, as the Little Spirits
are the forgivers.

Remember, with each step these Little Spirits take,

It is our job to make sure the path in front of them is a Red Road.

Remember, they are here as our teachers—

They trust, they believe us, but most of all, they depend on us.

These little ones are the ones that will wake a Nation.

These little ones will guide a Nation.

These little ones will lead a Nation.

These little spirits were us at one time.

Tobacco prayers go out to all who have entered this world. May each and every one of you walk on your pathway towards the Red Road your mothers have put before you.

An Ancestral Gift

Who am I?

What rights can I claim as a descendant of many Nations?

Why do I have to check a box of identity?

Why do I have to continuously prove myself?

Separation of identities isn't a private club requirement—or is it?

How can you express racism in front of your grandchildren, who carry the bloodlines of your anger?

When do we STOP using slang to refer to a painful past?

Are we the ones who continue the way of thinking that victimized our ancestors?

We can continue this conversation throughout time and the pain would not lessen.

What we need to do is identify the root of the anger that brings this conversation to the table.

Where there is prejudice, there is an inner hurt that is so deep inside us that we forget what really hurt us.

Our ancestors embraced people.

When they brought others into their homes, they
    became one Nation;

They became family.

When they loved, they embraced the bloodlines of
    many Nations and became one.

When they scolded another, it wasn't for what color
    they looked like;

It was for what they did wrong.

The true worth of our ancestors, and their beliefs, are
    being forgotten.

At our ancestors' table sat many children who had
    many Nations within them.

Our ancestors taught that to speak wrong about a
    person is to insult their grandparents too.

Our ancestors believed in living clean, being healthy,
    and care-taking the land we call home.

Our ancestors came in unique combinations of
colors, customs and cultures, but most of them passed
through life the same way, with love.

Our grandfather spoke to one of his grandsons and
    told him this:

"My son, you carry the beauty of many Nations and

with this, you carry many hereditary rights of wisdom. We are honored to call you grandson."

Then he smiled.

Our world today has become a society of private clubs with rules that exclude.

But we have freedom of choice and a bank of memories from our ancestors to draw on.

We can stand strong in their memory and say:

Today, we will make our ancestors proud.

Today, we will carry on their positive knowledge by embracing all life.

Today, we will live a healthy life.

When we are angry and upset with one another, the ancestors will help us find the root of this anger and speak solutions.

Sending tobacco prayers out to all to remember the ancestors. Remember them by looking at feet, hands and eyes, knowing that your feet are the past that stood strong, that your hands are the strength that pointed the way, and your eyes are the gateways of knowledge.

Finding *Gitchie Manidoo**

I find myself asking my ancestors for insight as to what will happen tomorrow. I need to know that my ancestors will be in our tomorrows.

Circles are everywhere, and it's the ones that keep spinning out of control that bother me the most. Sometimes I find myself getting stuck in these circles, and I wonder: *How do I get out?*

Today was a humbling day for me. I woke to my grandson lifting the daylight up out of the darkness and my ancestors whispering patience into my ears. I thank the resting place for keeping me warm and rested. Most of all, I thank the resting place for taking care of my body when I choose to soar with my ancestors.

My spirit rose above me onto Mother Earth's hairline, but my body stayed nested inside her soil, safe in the chamber of sleeping spirits.

I think I may have forgotten a lesson my ancestors warned me about. I don't know what could have distracted me from their powerful words of wisdom, but something did.

---

* *Gitchie Manidoo means Creator*

I walked today with three generations that come from me—what an honor. My daughter, who is now a mother—that is humbling in itself—my granddaughter, who brings new life to me each day, and my great-granddaughter, "Manidoo."

The littlest one will teach me the most humbling lesson of them all: the meaning of family. In this lesson, she will teach me the meaning of spiritual togetherness, the meaning of being wise, the meaning of being Native.

Each of us will experience doubt, which can bring out anger in each of us. l believe we have to experience this to understand what wisdom really is. Today, I am learning this lesson.

The day I am speaking of is a tale of sleeping spirits and tricksters who test you to the limit. Today, I felt like I went through all four gates of my religion.

We walked onto my homeland, my reservation, with happiness. We entered the Tribal building, a beautiful building, and we were met with happy faces, helpful spirits. There we were, four generations. Together, we waited for the Golden Key that would open the door to my family's longhouse, a space that whispers, "Welcome, you are home."

As we waited to be heard in this circle, we joked about the wallpaper, we read our Tribal newspaper, we had good conversation, we waited to be heard. A young Native girl called our names, and we went joyfully around the corner, down the stairs, and into a basement room. We were underground, in the nest of Mother Earth. Being there, I felt somewhat uncomfortable; normally this would not have made me feel this way.

My daughter, my granddaughter, my great-granddaughter and my other granddaughter entered this room. We were greeted by a Native man. He asked if we wanted something to drink. We replied "Mii gewitch—No, but thank you."

Three Native women were sitting in front of us, and two other Native women were sitting to the right of us. We were not sitting in a circle; our formation made the space look and feel like a courtroom. They read our plea to reconsider my great-granddaughter's enrollment as we brought evidence of her ancestry. They read that our great-great grandfather was a Chief who belonged to the Red Lake Band of Ojibwes. They stated that my grandmothers were from the Lac Courte Oreilles

(LCO), the Wisconsin Band of Ojibwes—they were both full bloods.

Then the hammer hit hard; it came from a Native woman. "NO; NO, NO," she said. "Manidoo cannot be enrolled; we will not identify her as one of our members; we do not recognize the Red Lake or LCO bloodlines." My heart stopped for a moment. I looked towards my descendants; they looked puzzled and sad.

For a moment, when I spoke, I felt an uncontrollable anger. Then my spirit re-entered my body. My words did not feel like my own, even as they poured out of my mouth: "Shame on you—shame on us! We shun our children at the doors of our longhouse and invite the non-Native in for food. What have we become? I need to leave this place; it is not a circle; it is pure craziness."

We left, got into the car and drove north. A few moments went by. As I sat, wiping my tears, I witnessed two Eagles soaring in front of our car— then two more came. My daughter was driving, and my granddaughters were in the back seat. Together, we watched these Eagles soar towards us and fly with grace all around us. Then, I heard a whisper. I rolled the window down and took a breath of fresh air. I stared at the *migizii's* —Eagles—and smiled. I understood their lessons.

The first Eagle will bring me the strength to understand our people and what we will become.

The second Eagle will bring me humbleness and caring for suffering spirits.

The third Eagle will bring me memories of the ancestors I feel are being disrespected.

The fourth Eagle was Grandma, all our mothers, reminding me that you do not need a paper to be who you truly are.

The whisper came from them. "We are in you, and we are also in her, and as long as you live, we live too."

The Eagles soared to and fro in all four directions. We watched all four of them soar over us. They lifted our spirits, embraced our hearts and reminded me of who I am and who they are. I closed my eyes, shed a few more happy tears, and spoke to my children.

I asked for forgiveness for my anger, and I said a prayer for the injustice of what had just happened. My six-year-old granddaughter asked why I was crying. I told her:

"When you ask for help and someone does not give it to you, don't be mad. Think of it this way: that person believes in you, and they know you can do it without their help. They want you to attempt whatever you are trying to do again. They know you will succeed, and that you will do it on your own."

I know this lesson might have been too complex for her little mind to comprehend, but I know her sister heard and understood this. I smiled at all of my beloved children.

That was the day I found *Gitchie Manidoo*. My great-granddaughter reminded me that we do not need a piece of paper in order to know who we are. All we need are our children, and their children, and their children's children. I looked at my great-granddaughter, Manidoo. She smiled, looked out the window at the four Eagles, kicked her little feet, and waved her little arms. She looked into my eyes—my spirit—and smiled.

The Identity Dance

It's not about knowing how to dance in this
exterior world,

It's about how freely your spirit dances within your
exterior shell, your body.

It's not about looking for identity to validate the dance.

It's about knowing that your spirit's soaring energy
can take you to the universe and back.

Many individuals get lost in identity today.

They carry many ancestral identities, or they don't
know how to find their identities.

Many will be silent and feel conflicted within
themselves,

Trying to know themselves and not live a false identity.

The simplest things, we choose to ignore.

The easier things, we will make difficult.

The mascots, the bullies, the tricksters,

The ones that need a title to describe their identities,

Are the most lost from not knowing themselves.

Stop. Listen to yourself, as you and only you have all the answers.

There was a plan prior to your entrance here on Mother Earth.

You knew your birth mother, while your body was taking shape around your spirit.

There was an environment you lived in that was your classroom until your feet felt the strength to stand alone.

There was a journey waiting for you, that gave you the negatives and the positives of life to teach you balance.

Who you are, all that you need to know, all that you long for, lives inside you.

Your spirit is your guide and your friend, giving you energy to keep moving on.

Every person who entered Mother Earth has a language, a tradition, a culture, a purpose, an identity.

Every person who feels lost, has forgotten their ancestors.

Every person who has a living grandparent, has an audio library.

Every person has free will, their spirit cannot be controlled even if their body is under lock and key.

Life is universal; we all need the essentials to live by: water, fire, air and food.

Life plays a melody of songs that we choose to dance to.

It might be lullaby, an instrumental tune, a hum, a sad song, a hip-hop song, a country tune or a love song.

Sometimes the dance we choose to identify with will be mistaken for who we truly are.

It's our ancestors' dance that we forgot, it's their foundation that we chose to wander from.

When we remember who they were, we will know who we are, and then we will be home.

Sending tobacco prayers out to all: To have a better understanding that the dance of life comes from our spiritual being, knowing that our exterior shell, our body, is just a blanket that keeps our spirit warm. To understand that to accept loneliness is to have a sleeping spirit. To know your ancestors, your foundation, your identity, is to truly know yourself, and the rest will happen.

Life is good today. Live it as a gift and unwrap your happiness one day at a time.

A Spiritual Journey on Mother Earth

A Creation Agreement starts from the spirit world.

A Creation Obligation happens with the first breath of Earthly life.

A Creation Appreciation begins with knowing the "We."

Creation never ends; it only moves on in the grand circle of life.

The seed of life is created from the union of male and female.

The basin of the cradle is made from the love of your mother.

The characteristics that develop are the result of what you hear and feel from the outside of this cradle.

The welcoming is witnessing the strength of a strong woman.

You suddenly adjust to a journey within Mother Earth.

You adapt to a classroom that is filled with choice.

You adopt all the relatives surrounding you.

You admire the two that gifted you this tunnel into this world, and then life begins.

It begins with love, laughter and warmth.

It begins with learning your challenges and learning your strengths.

It begins with learning to trust and learning to cry out for help.

It begins with experiencing your life's footprints, the DNA of your ancestors.

During life here on Mother Earth,

You will collect a mass of feelings and experiences.

You will learn balance, knowing what is right and wrong.

You will have choice without even knowing it.

You will become strong, a leader of your own Nations.

Then life will come to a close.

You will have the ability to see if you remembered your original agreement.

You will have time to process how well you did your duties here.

You will have a painted view of the journey you shared here as you turn around,

Seeing what you taught to all who watched you throughout life.

You will embrace the "We" within you and forgive yourself for living the "Me" during your time here.

Your agreement will read:

Thank you Father and Mother for planting the seed of the shell in which my spirit rested during this time here on Mother Earth.

Thank you, Mother, for carrying me with love.

Thank you, Father, for giving me strength and understanding.

Thank you, Ancestors, for all the journeys you made down to Earth to build the the pathway that we rest our feet on today.

Most of all, thank you for this spiritual journey here on Mother Earth.

This day of entrance is a birth entrance.

We will make an agreement of faith that we will cherish each step here,

Keeping the light on for the ones who need the light of hope.

Thank you, Mother and Father and all my grandparents, reaching back to the beginning of time, for this beautiful gift of life. To experience each day is a gift. It is a blessing to venture the world and experience the beauty of this home we call Mother Earth.

Family

Family:

To embrace such a thought brings you joy,

To enact such a measure of commitment brings you happiness,

To humble yourself to the endless needs of your loved ones brings you strength.

I look to the past,

I look to the present,

I look to the future,

I look to my family.

I did this; I made a family.

Most of all, they made my walk here on Mother Earth a joy.

A Grandmother's Awakening

My heart tells me to slow down,
My mind tells me there is much more to be done,
My body tells me to keep trying to go on.

My eyes fill with tears,
My hands are cold,
My feet want to run.

Our people are leaving,
Our wisdom teachings are fading,
Our Mother Earth and Father Sky are growing weak.

I reach for you,
I reach for them,
I reach for peace.

Then, our spirits awaken;
They dance, they dance, they dance.

Tobacco prayers go out to all who are awakening to
our peaceful dance. May you continue to carry your
grandmothers' teachings to our future grandmothers.

Extended Family

We had family night last night as we often do. My daughter and her father work for the police department, and it was Safety Night last night. What this means is the Holidazzle Parade in downtown Minneapolis invites all the firemen/women and the police officers' families. They signed our entire family up to be in the parade. All my granddaughters, grandsons, and my son were in the animal train float as giraffes and snow monkeys and mice. My youngest daughter portrayed Sherlock Holmes. They were all lit up—it was beautiful.

The weathermen were right on the money for once when they said it was going to be freezing cold, but somehow that chill was forgotten when the children arrived and joined the parade. My granddaughters waved like Princesses, smiling the biggest smiles ever. My granddaughter and grandson proudly and very protectively guided my son (who is medically challenged) down the street, smiling and dancing. I felt tears running down my cheeks, and the joy in my spirit began to dance.

After the parade was over, we all went to dinner. The little ones were hungry and exhausted. Even so, they sat there with the biggest smiles on their faces. The waitress asked what the special occasion was.

The birthday girl, my granddaughter, looked up and smiled, saying, 'We were in the Holidazzle Parade." The waitress said, "You watched the parade?" My granddaughter said, "No, we were *in* the parade!" Again, I felt the tears welling as I looked around the table of 15 wonderful faces, all in their own conversations, laughing.

The majority of my family is made up of what the system calls throwaway children from the foster care system. They were diagnosed as highly difficult special needs children with medical diagnoses so long and convoluted, it would take a medical dictionary to help me spell them out. Along with these little ones come their biological siblings, who we embrace with open arms. They too become our family and we are blessed to have them in our lives.

When times get tough and your children drive you crazy, take time to reflect. Close your eyes and think about one of the wonderful moments when they brought you joy. Life is worth the struggle; struggle is part of the journey.

Remember to give your love to a child in need. In the end, you will find that the child was not the only one who needed love and connection.

A Needless Battle

Yesterday I was in a meeting with a high government official. Thoughts were running through my head: What speech is she going to give us to please us and get us out of her office? But sometimes there are days that surprise you, and this was one of them.

I spoke about our foster care children and how society is quick to dismiss them, thinking, "they aren't going to be around that long, so there is no sense in investing in them." Then you run into people like this high official. Her voice is very strong within the school district, and I was wrong—very wrong—to go into her office and think my negative thoughts.

She spoke in a strong voice, asking me about myself and what I did. I told her what I did and voiced my opinions on what is lacking in the school systems for children in foster care. As I spoke, I watched her face turn into the face of a little girl, with powerful, passionate expressions.

She smiled when she spoke, saying, "I agree, I understand everything that you are saying. No one has ever told me of these situations. I want to thank you for bringing this to my attention and I want to share something with you. I grew up in the foster care system myself, and I never thought anyone cared about my struggles in school, never thought anyone understood me—until now. I will support anything that you think would be beneficial for these children."

I was in shock. I just sat there; I never expected this answer. I am so used to going into offices with a bag of problems and complaints, but I am not used to being heard.

I tell you, this is the season for receiving gifts and I just got one. I have been meeting people in high places that were either adopted or grew up in the foster care system. My spirit is full of happiness today.

No matter what your experience with a child, it only takes a moment to impact their little lives. So, when they act out, smile; they will remember that. Then give them their time out—you still have to be a teacher to them. These children are my life and my heart.

Tobacco prayers go out to all the children who think they are not wanted. May the Creator bless them with strength, happiness, dreams, and self esteem to last them a lifetime.

Consistency

Each waking day is a gift.

What we do in this passage of life will be remembered.

Our existence will leave a legacy:

Our children will be the manifestations of our teachings.

If we teach our children one thing and do another,

What are they learning?

If we teach greatness through our actions of goodness,

We raise leaders.

If we act angry without teaching where it comes from,

We cause the death of a Nation.

Sending tobacco prayers out to all the children and sleeping spirits to know the difference between being an angry person and being a good person.

Your Ancestors Live Within You

We carry our ancestors' DNA.
We carry our ancestors' behaviors.
We carry our ancestors' talents.
We carry our ancestors' strengths.

Have you ever wondered where your wisdom comes from?

Have you ever wondered:
When did I become so emotionally strong?
Where did all this talent come from?
Who taught me all this?

God, I don't know how I made it through that.
Dang, I learned that fast!
Geez, I can sing beautifully!

Wow, I just kept painting and painting—look at this
   beautiful creation!

I used to ask my Grandfather, "How do you know that?"
He would say, "Your ancestors live inside you and
when they want to come out, it is for a reason."

To help you when you feel weak,

To gift you their talents in order to amplify your own,

To teach you something they already know,

To awaken your talents,

To remind you that you are not alone in this world.

They live inside you,

They dance with your spirit to the rhythm of your
heartbeat, like the Big Drum.

Sending tobacco prayers out to all, to be reminded
that when we do something bad, it is not our
ancestors' doings. Rather, when we do something
bad, it is because our spirits are sleeping and we do
not know who is dancing inside our bodies. So stay
healthy, do not put anything bad into your vessel of a
body that houses your spirit and your ancestors, keep
on the Red Road of life. Breathe in Mother Earth's
breath and exhale your ancestor's journeys.

Life is good today.

Spiritual Shift

To recognize change, one must feel lost.

To discover a new beginning, one must mourn and let go.

To feel empty inside, one must accept new teachings.

To live life freely, one must be spiritually connected to themselves.

To stumble, one must be alert of their surroundings.

To fall, one must be willing to accept a hand in getting back up.

To cry, one must determine if the tears are spirit tears of cleansing.

To scream, one must know their own spiritual awakening, the "We."

To understand one's own spiritual shift, one must know their ancestors' journeys.

One must be able to understand that our breath is their breath,

One must be able to listen freely, to understand the whispers of the elders.

One must be able to sense in an Earthly moment the ancestors' journeys of yesterday.

When these moments happen, it is a spiritual wake-up call from our ancestors.

It is not that they are coming to us, they are coming from us, as they fear they are being forgotten.

They fear that their journeys of happiness, laughter and sadness will be lost.

They want you to look at your children, your people and yourself, to see the reflection of the journey of a people.

The elders say that in order for a spiritual shift to occur, you must take responsibility for your journey, the pathway that was set before you by Creator.

The elders also say that you can only be responsible for your own pathway, and that you are not to cross over onto the pathway of another, as this is not your journey.

Today, many people do not heed the advice of the elders and now many of our people are walking around in circles and can't get centered, so their balance is off.

Sending tobacco prayers out to all: Know your own pathways and do not forget your ancestors. Today is a good day to be "We."

The "We" Journey

When you live your life in the "I,"

Saying it's all about me, I deserve it, and so on,

You separate yourself from your inner spirit—you
disconnect.

The shell, your body, begins doing crazy things, while
your spirit sleeps.

You begin to walk a lonely path.

Time will move quickly in this world.

Slowly, your spirit will begin to awaken to all the
other spirit sparks that surround you.

They will shake you until you take control of this shell
of a body.

Your spirit will soar and begin to mend its shelter.

The spirit sparks will stay with you until they see you
glow brightly.

Friendship will become real between your body and
spirit.

Your body will ask for forgiveness.

Your spirit will embrace the connection.

Your journey will be restored and you will feel the
Red Road once again under your feet.

Your grandmother's breath whispers: "When you find
your way home and the adventure of 'me' is over,
you have returned to the 'We,' we are one."

Your grandfather showers your entire being, body and
spirit with all the elements it needs; he nurtures your
plant of a body with fresh water and rinses the poison
from your shell.

When you embrace the "We," you will begin to learn
the Creator's Story

As it once was told to you in the beginning of your
journey here on Mother Earth.

You will find the doorway to your shell of a body and
your beautiful spirit.

You will be reminded that the key, which you thought
was lost, was always with you.

You just needed to begin the relationship with yourself and begin to believe, as promised by our ancestors.

Sending tobacco prayers out to all who think they are lost...may each of you find strength to feel and see all the relatives around you in the form of their spirit sparks. Don't fear them as they are fighting for your spirit to awaken and for you to heal.

Life is good today; we are one.

We Are the Manifestations of Our Ancestors

To manifest is to wish for, to accept, to attract.

Our ancestors always believed in a better tomorrow
for their children,

And our children always wanted more for themselves.

Within these two messages, what is missing?

Our ancestors were living libraries of their ancestors'
stories.

Today our children can barely remember their great-
grandparents.

Within these two messages, what is missing?

Our ancestors had an appreciation for their home,
Mother Earth.

Our children cannot connect to their true
foundation.

Within these two messages, what is missing?

Our ancestors have passed on their abilities to
manifest peace.

Our children will fight over the simplest things and declare their ownership.

Within these two messages, what is missing?

What is missing is time.

Time is like a mirror, there will be a continued reflection.

It you don't take a moment to reflect on your life and think about the root of your being,

You lose time—you forget, you deny the beginning, you forget your ancestral journey.

You begin to manifest the negatives of life; you lose balance.

The interesting part of life is that it's never too late to learn,

To remember, to accept, to change, to continue.

To remember your ancestors is to manifest the positive,

To know a life a thousand years ago that your ancestors walked.

To appreciate a new day is to breathe your ancestors' breath.

Sending tobacco prayers out to all to awaken your inner spirit and manifest your ancestors' memories, to awaken to the positives of life, to bring balance back into your life.

Life is good today.

To Be Indigenous Is To Be Colorful

We live in the imaginations of our children.

We are teachers that will set an example.

We are the painters of the World.

We are the leaders of many Nations.

To be grand is to have journeyed a dark path and to
 have found a way out.

To be grand is to be remembered as a person with a
 kind heart.

To be grand is a gift to the generations.

There is a path that was paved before each of us was
 born.

There is a continued journey that each of us carries.

There is a responsibility that each of us must pass on.

There was a beginning, and there will be an end.

For each of us, there was a parent.

For each of us, there was a grandparent.

For each of us, there was a great-grandparent.

For each of us, history lives within us.

We all believe in Creation.

We will all create something or someone.

We all have a Creation story to pass on.

To understand life, we have to understand the four
    elements that Creator provides for us:

The gift of air, which is breathed into the body,

The gift of water, which nourishes the body,

The gift of fire, which keeps the body warm,

And the gift of food, which feeds the body.

Every person that walks this planet is Indigenous.

We are the children of Mother Earth.

There was a birthplace of our ancestors.

We all came from someplace we call our ancestral home.

There were many storms that our ancestors endured

to get here today.

There are many happy memories that have been forgotten.

Our elders are rising up once again; they do not want to be forgotten.

Our history is being erased—not by the hands of the wicked, but by our own hands.

We have become a blended people of privilege;

We have become warriors of a materialistic world.

Our expectations and our greed are destroying not only our family structures,

But our Nations.

We are harming the home we call Mother Earth.

Sending tobacco prayers out to all, to be reminded of this: Each of us holds the paintbrush of life. Without a colorful world, life is dim.

Ancestors' Messages

They say when a spirit surrenders their place here
on Mother Earth,

A portal is created between this world and the
spirit world,

Through which the living can hear the messages of
our ancestors.

They say these messages are meant to awaken the
spirits of the living.

In our ancestors' time, it was said that one of the
awakening prophecies

Would be thunder so loud it could flush the toxic
tears from the bodies that need it most.

They spoke of a yesterday that might be forgotten.

When this happens, our ancestors' cries will bring
big floods

From the bodies that house our spirits.

They say our bodies will be drenched in poison

That will try to keep our spirits asleep.

People will question our rules of life.

But our rules of life are written within us.

They say the waters that fall from the sky

Will beat down so heavily that it will make Mother
Earth upset.

They say the signs are all around us;

The night skies will no longer carry the beauty they
once had

And Mother Earth's wells will taste of bitterness.

They say mankind will cause unthinkable harm to our
four-leggeds,

And then to ourselves, as well.

Creation will come to a crossroads.

A prophecy is echoing throughout the world and very
few can hear it,

As we have forgotten our ancestors' message

That we must take care of Mother Earth and treat all
species with respect.

Time will no longer be a gift;

It will become a privilege.

They say the original plan to live in balance
   will become a test of mankind.

Sending tobacco prayers out to all who need to be
reminded: You must take care of your own space
first, plant the seeds of your children and tend the
communities around you. The rest will follow.

Life is good today. Walk in the pathways of our
   ancestors, knowing they are with us.

Photo by Marina Samovsky

II. SWIMMING IN TAINTED WATERS

When The Teacher Is Alcohol
and The Substitute Is Drugs

Innocence is what each of us is born with.

Privilege is a learned behavior; awareness is a gift.

Identity change is an honorable journey.

When an individual enters Mother Earth, they
    already know their journey;

It was written prior to their arrival.

Some Little Spirits will enter in a healthy shell of
    a body,

Others will swim in womb of toxic waters.

No matter the health of the body, the spirit will
    remain whole.

Life will educate many to be teachers of
    substance abuse;

Life will create many substance abuse classrooms
    throughout the world.

Life as we know it depends on the shells that house
    our spirits.

Life will also hide the doorways to recovery.

Time will stand still in a classroom of destructive
   teachers.

Life will feel heavy,

Life will become challenging,

Life will feel frightening.

When an alarm clock goes off within, the awakening
   will happen.

Life will become a doorway of choice.

Your diploma from the school of life will either take
   you on a journey of misery,

Or you will become a teacher of your own wisdom.

Aware that the journey you were on was not teaching
   you what you wanted to learn,

You will surrender yourself to a new journey,

Awakening your spirit to enter a new classroom of
   healthy teachings.

When your spirit awakens to that classroom bell,

You are ready to walk away from teachers you do not
want to be like.

Embrace your courage,

Embrace your weaknesses,

Embrace your challenges.

Embrace the classroom of LIFE!

We have a choice about what we learn in this world.

We can take back our own power and choose our own
pathways.

Sending tobacco prayers out to all: Remember that
you can become a teacher of life who does not preach;
you can be a living lesson of hope and happiness.

Addiction

Addiction occurs when someone enters the shell of your body, turns your light off, puts you to sleep and dances to a never-ending, devilish tune inside of you.

When you are acting crazy, ask yourself: *Would I have done that if I were of clean mind?*

Realize that you can stay awake.

When you learn how powerful the word "No" is, you just grew your Warrior Wings.

Tobacco prayers go out to all who need awakening:

And He will raise you up on eagle's wings,

Bear you on the breath of dawn,

Make you to shine like the sun

and hold you in the palm of His Hand.

Know that I believe everyone can awaken and grow strong, one day at a time.

An Old Way Of Thinking And A Celebration Of A New Day

Do you ever wonder why we have a New Year's celebration?

Do you ever wonder why we have a Winter Solstice?

Do you ever wonder why we overdo birthday celebrations?

Do you ever wonder why we go so overboard on Jesus' birthday?

Have you ever wondered, *Isn't every day a new one?*

Have you ever wondered, *Will climate change affect the Winter Solstice?*

Have you ever wondered, *Do we celebrate our lives? Do we give thanks to the life givers, our parents?*

Have you ever wondered, *How many people really know what Christmas is about?*

Do you ever wonder who benefits financially from our celebrating?

Do you ever wonder who suffers the most from these celebrations?

Do you ever wonder if the reason for celebrating has been lost?

Do you ever wonder how our ancestors celebrated, 200 plus years ago?

My father was born in 1889. When we were young, he and my older brother would share stories of yesterdays. One of the stories was about how people used to celebrate in the past. My father said, "We never celebrated in a self-centered way." He went on to remind us that each day was a spiritual gift to be appreciated.

My grandfather on my mother's side often spoke of "watching life from afar" to determine the worth of an event taking place. "If it is not involving a community in a good way," he said, "it's not worth the celebration!"

Our other elders spoke of the deceptive nature of celebrations, of community members using money they didn't have and walking away from their families to hide in the darkness of alcohol. Many people would celebrate to the point that they could not remember the celebration.

Our grandmothers used to describe what it meant to have healthy celebrations. They said these celebrations were full of laughs, feasts, and people united in ceremony together as one big family.

Have you ever thought about the day after the celebration?

Did it involve family in a good way?
Did you pass on good traditions or did you teach
  false happiness?
Was everyone happy in the celebration?
Will you do it differently in the future?

Not everyone will agree on what it means to have a
clean, healthy celebration of life. For those of you
who do walk in the good way and celebrate life with
goodwill, keep an open mind and an abundance
of prayers for the ones that walk in the shadows.
Ask Creator to awaken their spirits, so that they
can dance in the warmth of the good life as our
ancestors intended.

Life is good today. Remember, celebration does not
involve going broke or overdoing or over-consuming.
Sometimes, just being present and giving giant hugs
will seal the deal.

Sending tobacco prayers out to all: Celebrate life
one day at a time and remember that happiness is
always free.

Dark Alleys

There are many roads in this world.
Some take you to all the wonders of the world,
Some take you to a classroom of hard knocks,
Some take you to the dark alleys where we all fear
    to go.

The crazy thing is that we often choose the dark alleys,
We are curious to see what lies down those dark streets,
Where we meet the grandest of tricksters, who entice
    our very being.

These tricksters live in the alleys and come out to play
    in the light.

What is it that brings us out from those dark alleys?
Who turns on the light and shows us the way out?
When does a person say enough is enough?
Where are the exits from this dark place?

We all know the answers,
We all have the strength,
We all depend on guidance,
We all are aware of the tricksters.

I want to remind everyone, including myself,
    that there are tricksters amongst us.

Fear them not, just pray for them to awaken.
If you play their games, they win.

So, know those dark alleys,
Know those tricksters, they are all around us.

At times when our old trickster teachings arise within us,

Just recognize the behaviors as they are signs to
   "Be Aware."

Temptations are misleading.
Goodness is a lot of work.
Being bad is easy,
To achieve greatness, it takes a Nation walking side by
   side with you.

Tobacco prayers sent to get the trickster behavior
within us all to leave. Extra tobacco prayers to the
individuals who carry the teachings of these tricksters
and are not aware of it. I pray for them to totally
awaken and embrace life. Life is good, it's what we
make of our life and the teachings we leave behind
that will help carry the Nation forward on the bright
RED ROAD.

Blanket of Shame

This blanket is often heavy.

This blanket is often dark.

We can hide dirty stains of life in it, we don't have to
wash or clean it.

Most importantly, this blanket is mine, all mine!

What would happen if someone removed this blanket?

Would we get angry?

Would we fight to hang onto this blanket of shame?

Would we judge them for stealing our secrets?

Would we be ashamed if anyone finds out what's in
our blanket?

I tell you, don't wait for this to happen to you!

The anxiety and fear will poison your spirit.

Remember, everyone has their secrets, which
determine their destiny.

You can either move towards your future in fear,
or you can meet it head on and deal with it.

Did you do all the craziness with the help of drugs and alcohol?

Were you raised to believe that the craziness is normal?

What dreams did you have for yourself?

What was it that made you reach for this blanket?

The thing that will give you strength is awakening your spirit.

Your spirit has the warmth and strength to remove this blanket of shame.

Surrendering to the Creator and taking off this blanket of shame

Will lead you to the Red Road of courage.

Tobacco prayers go out to all who are taking their first steps. Remember, the past is the past; meet it head on, make your amends and then leave it behind. Today is truly a gift, so open your day and make happiness for yourself. Create a new blanket for yourself! Make sure it's bright, light and beautiful.

Chasing Craziness

What happens when I get so overwhelmed with daily
   demands?

What happens when I overextend myself?

When do I start to say no?

When do I admit to myself that I am exhausted?

How do I surrender to myself without guilt?

How do I ask for help?

When do I show the real me?

Who should I be afraid of?

I'm running as fast as I can.

I see you ahead of me, I'm almost there.

Just when I feel like I'm catching up with you,

You disappear, and then I am right back where I
   started from!

Am I chasing unreachable dreams?

The person I am chasing, could it be me?

Am I repeating myself?

Am I the one beating myself up?

This continuous fight that I have going on inside of me,

How do I stop it?

I want to live, I want to be free.

I want to stop chasing the pain and reach for
happiness.

Someone, please assure me that I am worthy!

Someone, please show me the path out of here.

Someone, please give me the name of the person who
has the key.

Could that someone be me?

Spirit Guides

I remember early on in my struggles with sobriety, I had very little support, until I ran into an Elder who told me this story.

She told me, "Look into water and see your reflection. When the water settles, look into your eyes; they are the windows to your spirit. Once you connect, you will wake your spirit and then think about a happy moment in the past to give your spirit something to hang onto, to keep awake."

The Elder told me that when we think about all the sadness and pain, we keep our spirits asleep, so we don't have to deal with them.

She told me that water represents life and the waves are the challenges we will be introduced to through this journey.

She reminded me that the only person who can teach you to swim is yourself.

Every wounded spirit has a spirit guide, she said, that lifts us up when we fall; but when our spirits are asleep, we choose not to see them.

She told me that you can find the strength to conquer life's disasters by having patience and waiting for the water to settle.

This is a task you will have to discipline yourself to revisit again and again, and to share with others.

She smiled at me and told me about smiling medicine, which encourages the spirit to want to stay awake.

That's why I give out smiles a lot, to keep me awake on my Red Road journey.

I have never seen this Elder again, but I know she comes and visits me when I rest this shell that my spirit lives in, as she did last night.

l believe her to be one of my spirit guides, so I pass on to you her teaching and many tobacco prayers to use when you need them.

The warrior in you becomes stronger when you reach out and ask for help.

In Whose Shell Are These Dancing Demons Partying?

Ever since I was little, I have seen them.
They would come and change all the people around me.
They made all these people look like they were having fun,
But little did they know that this vacancy they
    inhabited was only temporary.

These visitors to our bodies can be enticing—
They make you think you are having the best time of
    your life.
They are sneaky as they bring their other friends to
    steal your soul.
They put you to sleep and then the dance begins.

While you sleep, they advertise to the world that they
    are here.
While you sleep, they take you to dark places you
    would never travel to.
While you sleep, they trick you into singing hurtful
    words,
While you sleep, they multiply their victims.

These dark demons have no preference regarding
    gender, race or age.
They trick you into sleeping by using your so-called
    friends.

They tell you that you are on the best ride ever,
And they make you promises of endless joy.

Then, when these tricksters we call dark demons
 aren't looking,
Someone shakes you, someone leaves
 you a key,
These tricksters become aware of you waking and do
 the unthinkable.
They fight for your body, they want to end your
 walk here.

These tricksters forgot that their visit is only
 temporary,
They forgot that they will have to end the dance, they
 will have to go.
Remember when someone shook you awake and
 ended the dance?

It was you, only you.
You are the key, you are the way out.
You are free, you are free.
It's a new day.
But don't forget about those dark demon tricksters—
They will always be lurking!

Positive Growth, Finding Balance

When you find yourself in an uncomfortable
situation,

You can either jump into the craziness or you can be
silent for a moment to better understand that this is
not about you.

Which do you usually pick?

The craziness is not always about you.

When a person cannot understand their pain, they
will carry the weight until it gets so heavy they have
to drop it somewhere, maybe at your door.

Have you ever found yourself attracting mean
spirited people?

What was your reaction to their behaviors?

Did you join in on their craziness?

Did you think you were going to put them in
their place?

Did you linger on negative conversations?

Did you try to get other people to agree with your
reactions?

Did you break down and cry with resentment?

After all was said and done, how did you feel?

Life can be like walking on a tightrope.

We like the high of the adrenaline rush,

Not realizing that we have sensory disorders.

We forget that we have to know ourselves before we
can know others.

On the tightrope of life, I choose balance.

What I choose today will determine future feelings.

I will take responsibility for my actions.

I choose to be aware of not going into other
people's spaces

And not allowing others to stomp on mine.

Life is good today as I choose happiness!

The Awakening: Pain As A Career

Who is responsible for your life?

Who do you blame for all the hurtful bumps in your life?

What do you do when the pain is rooted so deeply?

What is it going to take to stop this merry-go-round lifestyle?

What happens when your secrets become an invisible weight?

What do you think will happen if you become pain-free?

Who knows of your hidden pains?

When will life offer you happiness?

You can repeatedly ask yourself these questions, and still continue to live a life weighed down by unhappiness.

When you start to wear masks that cover up your life's pains,

You begin to lose the real you.

You'll do anything to make the pain vanish.

What happens when you become so mean that no one wants to be around you?

What happens when even innocent children fear you?

What each of us don't realize is this:

We become walking billboards of our own pains,

We become a bullhorn, screaming, "Help!"

We become our own gatekeepers, keeping out our own happiness,

We lose ourselves and become imprinted by someone else's pain.

Time repeats itself, so pain repeats itself.

When we grow up, we can name the people that have hurt us,

We act out what our surroundings have taught us:

Our parents lost in alcoholism, drugs, and their own pain.

When we start to teach our children the pain we
    went through,

We become the teachers of repeated pain.

Time can heal us, one moment, one hour, one day
    at a time,

But we need help.

We need someone to help sort through all the
    garbage that we've collected throughout our lives,

We have to step back from our lives and bear witness
    to the pain.

When you realize that you are not alone in this
    journey,

When you own your pain,

When you stop shirking your responsibilities,

When you stop blaming,

Time becomes your best friend.

It's time to understand the beginning, our
    ancestral stories,

It's time to meet the sleeping spirits that rest within
    our bodies,

It's time to realize that all this worldly damage

happened to our bodies, not our spirits.

It's time to understand that even though you learned the lessons of a distrustful path,

There is another doorway that awaits, and it is called happiness.

The Red Road awaits on the other side of this threshold.

Sending tobacco prayers out to all: Know first that you are not alone in this journey. Life keeps moving, one step at a time, one day at a time. There are two of you—body and spirit. Your body and spirit have four directions of life to experience. Happiness awaits each of you.

Life is good today.

What Makes Me Cry

My first breath of life brought forth a tear of joy,

My first flood of tears brought forth a scream of
hunger,

The first time I tumbled out of balance brought
fear as my feet touched the ground,

My first expressions of loss came when you left
my sight.

The first time I left for school,

The first time I got lost,

The first time I got pushed down,

The first time I was called a name—

The list goes on and on.

There's always a first time.

What makes me cry

Is the loss of a loved one,

Or when a loved one hurts me.

What makes me cry

Is not knowing how to empower a loved one,

Not knowing whether to let them handle things
themselves.

What makes me cry is when I am rejected

For loving them the best way I know how.

What makes me cry

Is realizing that I was born into an alcoholic home,

Is knowing there was a better life for both me and my
parents,

Is not knowing what caused them to live like this,

Is knowing that I have to walk away from their pain

To live a better life,

To give them help,

And, most of all, to give them HOPE.

What makes me cry

Is seeing my loved ones coming through the doorways
of recovery,

Is feeling unconditional love without guilt,

Is understanding that life does NOT have to be
this way,

Is believing in a better life for all,

A life without hate, pain, and addiction.

What makes me cry

Is breaking the painful cycle,

Is seeing my children walking a wellness journey,

Is holding happy grandchildren,

Is feeling a beautiful, pure love from a great-grandchild,

Is knowing that the cycle of addiction was never
meant to be Iived.

Sending tobacco prayers out to all: Know there is a
good life out there waiting for you.

Life is good today.

A New Journey

When you bathe in a sea of tainted waters,
When you thirst for these tainted waters,
When you argue for and defend these toxins,
When you are no longer the real you....

When life is turned upside down,
When life is difficult to live,
When life becomes a burden,
When you forget about the beauty that exists in
this life....

Have you ever wondered what your life would be like
without alcohol?
Have you ever wondered what your life would be like
without drugs?
Have you ever wondered, *Why do I continue to do this?*
Have you ever wondered, *Am I all that I can be? Am I
happy—truly happy?*

What if the world never introduced these toxins into
our bodies?
What do you think that world would look like?
Would you have done all the things you did if you
weren't full of tainted waters?

When will someone warn the world that the
   most dangerous water of all, Alcohol,
   is legal and encouraged?

When will enough be enough?
Will I ever be able to beat the addiction?
Who will help me overcome the disasters of life?
What am I running to and running from?

Have you ever wondered, *Can I cheat life?*

The answer to all of the above is locked within the
   spirit that sleeps within your body.
The only one that can make change is you.
You, and only you, have the power.

Have you ever asked yourself, *Am I happy, really happy,
   with this life I designed?*

If you took time to read this and consider the
meaning of this message, that means change is in the
making. Validate the change that is emerging. Trust
your inner spirit. Your ancestors are telling you to
awaken to a life of beauty; they believe you are worthy.
Your journey awaits.

Strangers Among Us

There is a group among us that never shows
    prejudice—ever.
They embrace all walks of life, all ages, everyone.

Then the intruders appear.
They try to steal our members,
They invade our space with promises that go against
    our beliefs,
They turn the lights on when we enjoy darkness.

Some will be drawn towards this light,
Some will embrace them,
Some will leave with them.
But we know that you will return—
Remember: you are always welcomed home.

We look around at our membership and see that it is
    lessening,
We wonder why haven't they returned as they have in
    the past.
Where are they going?
Who are these strangers among us?

Here they come again.
My stomach aches with fear,
My mind is clouded with disbelief.

But I will go with them anyway,
Just to see who these strangers are.

I see many of the members from our old group—
They are smiling and embracing me.
Who are these strangers that feed my friends with lies?
I try to tell my friends, "Let's go back,"
But they do not listen.

I go back to my old group with my eyes somewhat open.
I do not see the smiles of my people;
All I see is pain.
They don't even know who I am.

Here come the strangers again.
This time, I will go with them willingly;
They remember me.
I am among my friends, who I once thought were
   strangers.

Now, I am one of those strangers, coming for you.
Our arms wide open,
With smiles to last a lifetime,
I am sober, I am drug free,
I am a survivor—they call me a stranger.

The Challenge

When we carry anger within our bodies, we become toxic. This toxicity prevents us from accessing our sanity.

It is possible to take two angry people who swear they hate everything about one another and guide them to peace. There are individuals out there who feel the need to find a target—to dominate, to enslave, to conquer—in order to find what they believe to be self-worth. We must learn to see this behavior as a billboard, an announcement, a cry for help.

What about the ones that welcome the role of being a victim? Have you noticed that these people tend to keep themselves in the same place? Who taught them to be helpless? When did they lose their self-worth and replace it with silence or raging anger?

Think about the fire that is raging within your body; identify where it came from. Is there a possibility of a calm after the storm? *Where do I start to ask for guidance, to seek help, to find balance?*

We all came from the same doorway of life. *Could my personality have come from the moment I was conceived, from Day One in my mother's tummy? What was her life like? What was she feeding me during my nine months in the womb? From Day One of life, was I taught by a broken human being? Did I sprout from a dysfunctional community, a toxic society?*

To find balance, we must remember our seven generations' journey and the fresh waters, healthy vegetation, and pure oxygen that we need to live healthfully on Mother Earth.

Honor a Woman, Honor Life

Understand this: you cannot draw milk from an undernourished cow.

You cannot feed from Mother Earth if you continue to pollute her.

You cannot drink from her waters if you continue to contaminate her veins.

You cannot beat a woman and wonder why she is broken.

Remember, no matter all her shortcomings or her virtues,

Life cannot exist without the existence of the feminine.

To honor a woman today, no matter her faults,

Is to honor Life for the Nations yet to come.

Tobacco prayers go out to all who have witnessed anger towards women, and extra for women to awaken to a world that awaits their return.

Life is good today.

Who's Fooling Who?

Like everyone, at one time or another, you have been consumed
By anger and blame at the shortcomings of others.
You have screamed to the world, *They made me do it!*

You have struggled within yourself, believing you are worthless,
Thinking, *No one likes me!*
You have crossed the line of insanity,
Lashing out verbally or physically at others because they made you mad.

What if you were born into a world of alcoholism and drugs?
What if your body struggled within your mother's womb,
A womb that was filled with alcohol or drugs?
What if some parts of you were not fully developed?
What if...?

Have you ever said, *"Nobody is going to tell me what to do!"?*

Have you ever been beaten because they love you?

Have you ever spent your rent/food money on "going out clothes" or partying?

Have you ever had difficulties with learning?

Have you ever found yourself doing things because someone told you to?

Have you found yourself remorseful after doing the unthinkable?

Have you ever found yourself in an illegal situation, wondering, *How did I get here?*

Have you ever been so preoccupied that the real world passes you by?

The list goes on.
The result never changes; it only gets worse.

Do you ever wonder, *how can I change my way of life?*
What if I change and don't like my new world?
What if I go back to the old ways?
Do you ever feel like you need someone to help you move through the craziness?

If you have had any of these wonders, you are healthier than you think....

There is a small hole inside you that showers light from within.

It is called your spirit.

You first entered this world as a spirit, as pure,
   beautiful energy.

You entered a body and world that were broken.

It is balance you long for—to live happy, healthy, and
   most of all, safe.

My father used to say: "The only fool in a situation is
you. No one put you in a bad situation; no one made
you do it. No one cares if you live or die. If you mess
up, no one is going to bail you out—no one; not if you
are just going to do all this again and again."

He would tell us that we were the only ones who
   could make things happen.

He taught us about self-ownership.

Even when you feel shame, remorse and loneliness,

Even when you are in an environment of
   unhealthy living,

You still have light within you.

Embrace this dimness within you and walk towards
   the light;

It will get brighter.

The brightness will lead you out of this dark world,

Because this light is you.

When you realize the foolish games that you embrace,

You can honestly say, *I am the fool of my own foolishness.*

Recognizing this truth will give you balance when you encounter another dark situation.

Remember to embrace the "We," the sacred pair, spirit and body.

Remember that we are never alone, as we carry our ancestors within us.

Remember that your first love must always be yourself.

The Spiritual Bank

What happens when you have all the exterior riches
in life and you still feel lost, lonely and unhappy?

My grandfather once told us, "A rich man has nothing
to give other than a spiritual blessing, from one good
spirit to another."

The women in our family would speak of their wealth
from an ancestral knowledge that was handed down
to them. The Grandmothers concluded this lesson by
whispering:

"Be careful what you wish for if your wishes are not
    for your spiritual enrichment."

The men in our family would not speak of their
wealth other than to show the kindness from within
them; they told us that this is the real gold mine.

Our children have learned of the richness of life from
their families, but society has also influenced their
understanding of wealth. Society causes us to have
delusions about what it really means to be rich.

Family values are sleeping as the alcohol and drugs
    sweep the bodies of our people.

The children of today fight amongst one another

and claim one another as property, saying "He's mine" or "She's mine." The conversations of today are full of bickering, finger pointing and evasion of responsibility.

Today, we struggle to be happy.

Today, we expect money to make us happy.

Today, we have fallen victim to a society that is full of illusions.

There is a break in the musical chain.

First, the rhythm of the Mother Earth's heartbeat,

Next, the rhythm of Life's pulse,

Last, the confusion of what channel to listen to.

We keep switching the channels of life,

As if it were the radio in the car or the instrument in our hand.

We are never pleased to just listen.

Where are the Grandparents' voices of yesterday?

When did Life change?

Since when does Love come with a price tag?

Sending tobacco prayers out to all to know that happiness, true happiness, is when your inner spirit—the battery that is keeping this shell of a body moving—is acting in your best interests.

Sending prayers for strength, for balance, and for recognizing when deceptions come into your life.

Sending prayers for healing, for forgiving yourself, for never forgetting that your ancestors are still around, for never forgetting that they live inside you.

The last of these tobacco prayers is to know when to withdraw from the falsehoods of life and get back to real life; to drink the pure waters and not the tainted waters; to recognize the sleeping potions that keep your spirit asleep, and to choose to stay awake.

Life is good today.

Return to the Water Gatherings

There was a time when the gathering of women
Meant support, laughter and learning.
When did this trust start to vanish?

Where has all the trust gone?
When did we become so angry with one another?
What have we taught our daughters and sisters?
Who was the teacher who taught us all this negativity?

I have an idea, and it goes like this:

As we wrestle with all the problems of today,
As we allow ourselves to carry this craziness,
As we forget about those happy moments,
We forget all those happy teachings we once learned.

There was a time when we all went to the waters and
laughed,
There was a time when we all prayed for the waters,

There were times when these waters washed away
everything,
There were times when these waters were blue.

Either way, we have a choice,
Either way, we can remember,
Either way, we can relearn,
Either way, we can start to feel that happiness again.

Remember your journey,
Remember your mother's journey,
Remember your grandmothers' journeys,
Remember your great-grandmothers' journeys.
Remember.

Warning:
Be careful what waters are put into your body,
Be careful of the tricksters that are serving you,
Be careful of the taste that will entice you,
Be careful not to let it change your path.

Remember the pure waters,
Remember the laughter,
Remember the trust,
Remember, the healing has begun.
We will become one again.

Swimming in Tainted Waters

There was a time when we sat in council with freewill,

There was a time when our voices were joined together,

There was a time when life was lived with love and laughter,

There was a time when our spirit lived in a healthy
blanket of a body,

There was a time....

Our ancestral prophecies have never left us;
each of us just misplaced our lessons.

Our Elders spoke of a day when a war would happen
that many would surrender to freely. They said, "This
war will deposit a poison in our water that will swim
among us; it will put our spirits to sleep, and when
this happens, we will be defeated."

Our ancestors' voices, though faint, remind us that
our spirits used to enter Mother Earth and swim in
the purest of waters, our Mothers' wombs. Then,
there was no alcohol among us.

They say we will come to a broken path, at the end of
which will be a pool of beautiful waters that will be
deceitful and poisonous. They speak of the dangers of
getting lost in this world. When this happens, Creator
will send Spiritual Warriors to wake the sleeping
spirits that fell victim to the poisoned waters.

Alcohol has done horrible damage—our communities
   can testify to this.
Alcohol has silenced our inner spirits; it has put us
   to sleep.
Alcohol brought company with it, and this company
   is called drugs.

The battle against alcohol and drugs can be won,
But it will take 100% of our effort and commitment.

Indigenous Elders all across the globe are saying,
   It is time.

The true Ancestral Warriors will start to appear, and
they will go into battle with the strength of their
ancestors. They will remind us that their ancestors
did not fight a war to get us here so we could live like
this. The awakening is happening—the Warriors are
appearing all across Mother Earth, in the tradition of
our ancestors.

Sending tobacco prayers out to all: Do not shun
these emerging warriors; they are trying to make
life better and make sure our lives are lived as our
ancestors intended.

A Native Story

The Creator gathers all the animals and says, "I want to hide something from humans until they are ready for it: the realization that they create their own reality."

The Eagle says, "Give it to me. I'll fly it to the moon."

"No, one day soon they will go there and find it," the Creator says.

"How about the bottom of the ocean?" asks the Salmon.

"No, they will find it there too," Creator replies.

"I will bury it in the great plains," says the Buffalo.

"They will soon dig it up and find it there," Creator says.

"Put it inside them," says the wise Grandmother Mole.

"Done," says the Creator. "That's the last place they will look!"

What a valuable lesson this is for human beings. To find your own reality, you must look inside yourself, with Creator's help.

Photo by Jane Feldman

At a gathering of several Global Wisdom Grandmothers in Times Square, New York City, Grandmother Doreen Bennett, Maori from New Zealand, greets Ojibwe Elder Great-grandmother Mary Lyons. The traditional Maori greeting, the *Hongi*, is done by pressing one's nose and forehead, at the same time, to another's. It is used at traditional meetings and major ceremonies among Maori people and serves a similar purpose as a formal handshake. In the *Hongi*, the *ha*, or breath of life, is exchanged.

III. FINDING BALANCE

Ownership

The world around you is of your own making.

If there is chaos, then you feed off it.

If there is happiness, then you created it.

If there is both, be careful that you don't fall.

When you wake with the day, be thankful for this gift.

What you do this day will follow you forever.

Who you connect with today is of your own choice.

Wherever you choose to journey, don't forget that you are leading the way.

Seek out your dreams, look for laughter,

Trust in the ones that have contagious smiles.

Believe in yourself, knowing that you have contributed to change today.

Remember, life is short, dreams are big.

Remember to live your life and not someone else's.

Live your life happily and make at least one dream come true for yourself today.

Sending out tobacco prayers to all to believe in this gift of life and to know that they make life happen for themselves.

Balancing Act

Do you know why you get headaches?

Do you often have aches and pains?

Do you often feel depressed?

Do you often look for negative energy?

My father once told me that when you don't have balance in your life, your body will alert you. You will either experience all of the symptoms above, or maybe a heart attack—just about anything that will get your attention.

What you need to do is identify each ache and pain, find out when it started, and then revisit again. My father said it's important to be aware of all your daily anxieties, paying attention to who or what triggers them.

My grandfather would call these dark moments: moments when the dark spirits tried to get your attention so you'd play with them. This scared me!

My father said we lack balance. We misuse our medicines; we laugh at all the wrong things. When we make fun of other people, we make ourselves sick. We have forgotten what laughter was supposed to be about.

When I learned this lesson and started to change my life, things began to change for the better. My health became better, my shell of a body became well.

Good balance comes from good laughter, good smiles, good words.

Happiness gave me good health and good balance.

Tobacco prayers go out to all who need to learn their good balance.

Stinking Thinking

Do you ever find yourself arguing with nonsense?

Do you ever feel the world is out to get you?

Do you find yourself playing victim?

Do you keep repeating and getting the same results?

Do you ever stop and analyze what just happened?

Do you ever think you can change a person's ideas to your way of thinking?

Do you find yourself judging others much too often?

Do you feel you are always stuck in the same old conversations?

Do you find yourself year after year feeling you live in chaos?

Do you ever dread your day when you wake?

Do you ever dread the people you are amongst?

Do you ever want change?

Well, my friends, if you answered yes to all the above as I did,

You are in for a great change in your life.

Being a grown-up with grown-up responsibilities means work.

Change comes from within, not from trying to
   change others.

Just think about all the energy you waste, trying to
   convince others of your values.
What you need to do is stop this lifestyle.
STOP IT!
Stinking thinking is wasting your gift of life.

Look around, really look around, assess your
   surroundings.
Do you find yourself knee-deep in negative energy?
Walk away, heal yourself before you attempt to
   heal others.
Just know it took you time to get to this place,
So it will take some time to get you out.

Remember, when you shine with healthy thinking,
you create a pathway of light that many will follow.
When you let go of the garbage backpack, life will
feel so much lighter.

Tobacco prayers go out to all for self-insight and
   healing.

Overworked

Why is it so easy to be bad?

My father told me to really think about this word
    "BAD."

Then he told me what his mother, Josephine Lyons,
told him—that BAD means "Being Always Desperate."

"When you are left in this world alone, you will do
just about anything to be heard and noticed. Each
person has this sense of desperation in them, it's an
overpowering need when you are lonely," Grandma
Josephine said.

Why is it so hard being good?

Why do you have to put so much effort into this action?

Why are the benefits so much less than being bad?

Who are we trying to please with this behavior?

When I needed to hear a mother's voice, Hazel
    White-Hare, my beloved Aunt, told me this:

We are blessed to have this journey,

We are blessed to take each step on these paths;

We were gifted with strength like no other,

We have to pave a path for the Nations behind us yet to come.

We can either teach the craziness or we can help change life for our people.

She said, "Think about the word GOOD. It's God's name being shouted your way. When we yell for you children to come to us, we stretch your names so that you hear us. This is just how God wants you to remember your path here as he has faith in you."

To all the good people who have walked before me:

I will do my best to be GOOD and remember that the Creator has faith in me to help lead Nations yet to come. I will embrace my shortcomings and ask for help when I sense "BAD" feelings coming over me. I appreciate my overworked life. I am not alone; my Grandmother Josephine, my father Charlie and my precious Aunt Hazel rest in my inner spirit and they believe in me.

Life is good today.

Patience in the Face of Confusion and Frustration

Each day is no different than the day before if you choose not to change it.

Lessons in life can be like potholes in the road.

Each time we go down this road, we get annoyed and complain, wishing someone would fix it.

Have you ever wondered why we keep repeating things that annoy us?

Have you ever thought at the end of the day, *life is cruel?*

Have you wished you could change another's behavior?

Have you ever felt frustrated at having your commands or entreaties ignored?

We have all gone down this road at one time or another.

The key question is, what makes us get off this damaged roadway?

Frustration can be like a blindfold, if we choose not to remove it from our lives.

Patience is plentiful and yet many of us choose not to make use of it.

Have you ever turned around and looked at your
   life and seen chaos?

Have you felt like you need to be above everyone
   else to be safe?

Have you ever felt like just giving up?

We all have at one time or another; that's life.

If you're standing in craziness, walk out of it.

Many will say "That's easier said than done," and
   continue to live in turmoil.

Others will seek the patience to figure a way out,
   and then they'll move on.

BAD things will happen to us

If we choose to continue wandering down this
   damaged road,

Blaming others for all our shortcomings.

Why? Because it's the easy way out.

 It's called CONFUSED FRUSTRATION.

Try to remember this short, simple key word: BAD.

It stands for:

Being

Always

Desperate.

Now try patience and seek a better path in this lifetime.

Sending tobacco prayers out to all: To stop for a moment and examine your life, then look down at your feet and make the choice to either stay in the crap or walk away.

Also sending more tobacco prayers out for healing and strength, as all of us need it. No one is better than the next, but some choose to walk away from the garbage they are standing in.

Life is what you make of it. Being responsible for your choices is your reward at the end of the day. Remember, you are worth the happiness that awaits you.

Smiles and Laughter

Laughter can be medically rewarding, if you share
your laughter in a healthy manner.

Laughter can be cruel, if you choose to laugh at
someone in a negative manner.

Laughter can be easily mistaken as harmful, if you
choose to go into someone's space, demanding
'WHAT ARE YOU LAUGHING AT?' without
being there from the beginning.

Laughter can be sparked by the action of a little one,
as well as by the eldest person on the planet.

Smiling can be rewarding to the spirit and the world,
if the intention is healthy.

Smiling can be harmful, if you look at a person with
an unhealthy intention.

Smiling can change a person's attitude either way,
making them angrier or making them feel happy.

Smiling can be sparked by the action of a little one,
as well as by the eldest person on the planet.

It's what is in between that counts.

When your body laughs or smiles, it's very different from a spiritual smile or laugh.

Have you ever had someone look at you in a creepy way and smile?

Have you ever felt uncomfortable when someone laughed at what you just did?

Our grandfathers would tell us that it's how you respond to others' actions

That determines your spiritual value.

Our ancestors would tell us not to waste our energy by gifting another with cruel intentions.

"Don't laugh at a person who made a mistake; you'll get it back 100 times worse!"

Never smile falsely, "wanting something in return."

Our ancestors remind us that self-centeredness can lead you to waste the best medicine in the world: smiles and laughter.

You will end up making yourself sick.

Remember, the gift of laughter is from your inner spirit; it's good medicine.

The lesson here is simple:

Check yourself when you laugh, when you smile.

Be a teacher of goodwill; do not join in hurtful laughter.

Remind others not to acknowledge smiles that lead to something other than goodwill.

Most of all, be the teacher who teaches children to know the difference.

Let your smile change your environment.

Let your laughter send a peaceful rhythm throughout the world.

Now, can you feel your face smiling and your inner spirit dancing with joy?

Sending tobacco prayers out to all: to spread healthy smiles and wonderful laughter, knowing the difference between goodwill and bad intentions.

Life is good today.

Mending The Family Circle

What happens when you feel disconnected from a
    family member?

What happened that contributed to this mess?

Will there ever be a moment when each of you will
    be heard?

What are you up against that is so painful?

Why do they treat me so badly?

When did we lose our way?

What makes me so angry?

When did they change?

How do we get back to a healthy relationship?

Who will take the first step?

Who else is being hurt by our behaviors?

How do we ask for help?

These are important questions to validate.

Life is like a movie:

Romance, we remember every detail.

Tragedy, we express our tears.

Mystery, we get totally involved.

Comedy, we share in the laughter.

Horror, we hide in fear.

Afterwards we laugh together about getting through it.

What if you take a moment to write the movie of
your life?

When did your nightmare begin?

What details do you want to make known?

Who are the other actors in this story?

Most importantly, how did it end for you?

What's amazing is that you can change the ending.

You are the writer and the director of your own movie.

And you are not the only actor in your production.

Now, for the critics....

You will always be your own worst critic.

It may feel like the world is against you.

As you awaken you may feel like you are still in the
horror movie and you cannot push STOP.

But here come the credits, and surprisingly your name
fills every slot.

By taking responsibility for your own life, you
create a new direction.

You and only you will create change.

What may be sad is this: you might be the only one
to change.

Starting your new journey might mean leaving
many you know behind,

As they may not accept your new reality.

This pain will be real.

You might even hope you can change their minds.

Then the reality hits hard; we each must write our
own life script.

Sending tobacco prayers out to all.

Judgments

To measure another's shortcomings
Is one less moment of your time to be wonderful.

So to all who find themselves blaming others for
    what their life is about,
STOP IT!
Stop handing out your control.
You cannot change others, you can only change
    yourself.
Value your time today, value yourself.

If you see and feel the frustrations of others,
Close your eyes and ask the Creator to give you
    strength not to judge,
Then smile and leave their space.

At the end of the day, ask yourself, who or what took
    so much of my time today that did not feel good?
Don't just look at the moment of frustration,
Look at the entire picture.
Just know that you don't have the power to judge,
Only the Creator does.

Other people walking the dark road will test you
 daily,

They will come for you in many ways.

Remember, their spirit is sleeping;

You don't really know who you are dealing with.

Know them, know yourself, be strong, smile and
 offer a kind word:

"Sorry that you are having a bad day, hope it gets
 better, you are worth it."

It just might wake them.

Hand out positive energy and you will fill your
 spirit with happiness.

If you find yourself trying to convince someone
 that your way is the best

And it's not working, RED FLAG, stop.

Lead by example.

Tobacco prayers for strength to know what battles are
worth it, and to fight in a positive way.

Be your own teacher for the day

There are teachers among us.
Be careful what you learn and who you learn it from.
No one can make you crabby, you do it all on your own.
Just know that you mimic others' behaviors by choice.

So today, surround yourself with good teachers,
The ones that make you laugh and feel good.
Or be the teacher today and spread the good
   medicine around,
Pass out smiles instead of sour facial expressions.

Tobacco prayers go out to all who need a smile today.

Emptiness and Doubt

When we entered Mother Earth

We were gifted with life, love, learning and trust.

Many were gifted with healthy bodies, while others weren't.

Many were gifted with healthy families, while others weren't.

Many were gifted with awesome communities, while others weren't.

Each of us, no matter the circumstances, was gifted a bag within us to fill with knowledge.

Each of us, no matter our conditions of living, was gifted a mind that is ours to control.

Each of us, no matter the company we kept, was gifted a magnet of loving energy.

Each of us, no matter the environment, was gifted the instinct to choose wisely.

While journeying on Mother Earth, confusion will cross our paths.

Many say it's a crossroads of life, put there so that you will have the chance to choose which way you will journey next.

At these crossroads of life, whether it be choosing the right mate, where you will work or where you will live, there will be a bit of doubt, wondering if you made the right choice.

Within each passage, you will begin to feel the weight of life on your shoulders and you might wonder "what is this empty heavy weight that I carry?"

You will begin to feel more weight as you doubt your choices and become lost within your existence. Your pathway disappears.

Then, the introduction happens.

We came into a world of expectations, needs, wants and even demands.

We came into Mother Earth's home without proper introduction, permission or obligation.

We became arrogant as we grew within her home and demanded Father Sky to shine on us at all times.

We forgot or were not taught the proper etiquette of entering.

For a moment, think about how you would feel if someone barged into your home, demanding and expecting this and that from you and you don't even know them.

Now, embrace those feelings, write them down, look at them, study them.

Then ask yourself this: Was my entrance to Mother Earth a welcoming one?

Think about the weight of emptiness and doubt that you carry.

Now is the time to reenact this greeting by asking Mother Earth for forgiveness and properly meeting her.

Teach your children to lessen the weight of disparities.

Teach them to walk equally next to one another and never to feel they are better than the next, just as Mother Earth and Father Sky do not treat one more favorably than the other.

Their expectations are this:

You are welcomed into our home as long as you respect, love unconditionally, treat mankind as your brother and take care of us as we will take care of you.

If you forget this law of nature, you will be reminded with more weight of emptiness and doubt that will drive you to thinking and staggering on many uncertain pathways.

Sending tobacco prayers out to all: To be reminded that we do not own Mother Earth, though we may pay rent while we are here. Be reminded that a man's riches are only measured by a corresponding amount of kindness.

Life is good today. Thank you, Mother Earth and Father Sky, for allowing me one more day in your home.

Bad Medicine, Bad Karma, Bad Choices

Exterior living is real and what you send out into
    the Universe, you get back tenfold.

This is the "Me" thinking: it's all about me.

Interior living is a spiritual journey and what is
    unique about this is:

No one can touch your spirit, no one.

If someone wishes bad stuff on you,

They can only make it happen if you accept it.

Spiritually, you can overcome anything;

You are a Warrior of this journey here on Mother Earth.

Believe it, see it, feel it, own it.

There will be obstacles in your path and these are
    called lessons of life.

Once you make it through these lessons, they turn
    into Wisdom.

To find BALANCE, live in both worlds—spiritual
    and material, interior and exterior.

This is the key to living in harmony,

Getting rid of all the bad that may be thrown your way.

This is living in the "We."

The body is a blanket that houses your spirit, a
    DNA imprint of your ancestors' journey.

Here on Mother Earth, your spirit is your
    ancestors' energy,

Combined into one body that carries you through
    all the good and bad

And back into the balance of the "We."

Remember, if someone throws bad medicine at you,

You can either accept it, or know it bounced off you.

It's a choice.

Many might disagree with this and continue to own
the negatives that have become a comfort zone for
them, giving them reason to react the way they do.

Or they may not understand their own spiritual power.

Remember, if you say bad karma will come back on you,

It's like sending bad medicine onto another.

Wishing something negative on to another, makes
    you part of the negative.

This is exterior thinking.

Remember, if you make bad choices,

That only shows that you are in a bad place; you
are crying out for help without even knowing it.

Most people will argue this to the point of crossing
the line and getting physical with another person.

The key to avoiding this violence is knowing not
to feed the predator that awaits in the darkness of
your soul.

Our grandfather would teach us that BAD (Being
Always Desperate) is so much easier than working
hard at being good!

He would say, your behavior as a person will show
your true spiritual growth as an honorable descendant
of the Wisdom Keepers.

Sending tobacco prayers out to all: To know you are
the strength, you are the Warrior, you are a Wisdom
Keeper if you live within your spiritual being.

Life is good today and being a forever student is
honorable.

Pedestal Thinking

All through life, we have the tendency to worship
    others.

We put them on a pedestal for what they think and do.

If asked "What makes this person so worthy?"

Most will talk about their achievements and
    goodwill.

But what if you find out that the person you
    admire most

Is full of shortcomings and failures?

Would you defend their worth?

Would they do the same for you?

My father often said to us, "When you find yourself
spending so much of your day defending others, what
does that say about yourself?"

This always made us think and we would say,

"Cuz, they're our friends."

He would tell us that it wasn't our job to be a referee.
"The conversations out there don't have your name in
them, so why include yourself where you don't belong?"

My father would listen to debate but one thing he did not allow was going into negative conversations without the person we were talking about being there.

He said, "It's a waste of time to gossip, that's a mean person's game, not to mention a weak person."

He would tell us that other people's doings are just that, theirs.

Strong people would have a conversation with the individual, not with the world that this person isn't in.

When you go into a debate, it's important to discuss solutions, not just argue over who's right or wrong.

When my grandfather spoke and said "No," that was it, we did not question him. We just trusted his decisions and they were always right.

If he knew we wanted to play with and follow mean people, he would tell a story of when he was little and his mother told him, "If your friend stood on a skinny branch over the rough river, you would go stand next to him? Now, who's the friend and who's the dummy?"

My father and grandfather would often ask us, "Would you feel scared to confront the person that you are whispering about to others? Then you have no business having this conversation; it's a waste of a good day."

We were taught that people don't climb up on these pedestals themselves; other people, with low self-worth, put them up there.

To respect another's values means to walk side by side with them and feel the same respect back.

Today I teach my children and grandchildren our ancestors' lessons of life. When an elder tells you "no," understand the full meaning behind it. When they tell you "yes," be prepared for values to live by.

Sending tobacco prayers out there to understand and appreciate the ancestors' voices and to start having good conversations.

Powerlessness vs. Empowerment

When you are a child, you feel powerless.

When you learn from this sense of powerlessness,

You most likely will repeat the life that was set before you.

When will you learn that you can change your life?

If you had a healthy childhood,

Someone taught you to be empowered, to make good choices.

What happens down this road of life, when you go down a dark alley?

Do you turn your empowerment into feeling powerless?

As a young adult, you feel you can conquer anything,

As an adult, you are not so sure.

As an Elder, you should know the difference between empowerment and powerlessness.

But what if you don't?

Be alert to familiar or unfamiliar faces with hidden agendas.

When someone tells you what you are doing wrong,

Listen to them and ask "how can I do things differently?"

It is up to you to either live powerless and stuck in your old surroundings,

Or to take back your power and create a new world for yourself.

You are the only one who can tell your body to breathe.

Life is free; it's a gift, it's yours and yours alone.

You can choose how to live your life.

If you love it, live it.

If you hate it, change it.

You have the power to breathe life,

So, now go live it...happily and healthily.

Tobacco prayers to all who need the reminder that they hold the power of life. May they meet their fear head on and take back their power.

I Am Who I Am Today, By Choice

Being angry today only validates the teachings of the intruders.

Being dismissive today only validates your tell-tale signs of pain.

Being physically violent today only validates what you learnt well

From the negative teachers of hidden pain.

Being absent today only validates the sleeping spirit within you.

When you become aware of your negative behavior,

You are hearing the ancestors within you, saying, "Enough with this."

Remorse for your negative actions is your spirit awakening.

Wanting to learn more positive outcomes is your spirit seeking balance.

Seeking out wellness is coming home to the real you.

Life is a classroom that often is full of tricksters.

Life can teach you to either live in a negative or positive world.

Life can either be a walk in beauty or a silent place of pain.

Life is a gift, it's a choice, it is your choice—it's up to you how you want to live it.

Today is a new beginning, you can either live like you hate

Or seek what you want, what brings the real you to life.

Sending tobacco prayers out to all to awaken their inner spirit, rejoice with their ancestors and live to the fullest.

Life is good. Today is a good day to start to live a life of happiness.

Today's Adventures

Today is about today.
If I think about what happened yesterday without
    enjoying this day
It validates that I did not take care of my business at
    that time.

If you keep passing on today's adventures
By staying with yesterday's mistakes or regrets,
You are just chasing your own tail of unhappiness.

How do you get past this?
Make a list of what bothers you, things that keep
    resurfacing.
Set an hour out in the middle of the week and deal
    with those things.
Then let them go.

Just remember, if we keep dwelling on the past, we
    will forget to live in the present.

Sending tobacco prayers out to all who need to
remember to live today: make a bunch of laughter,
then move forward. Don't be one of those people who
thinks life is forever. Wake to reality and live happy
and healthy, making good memories that you will
share when you reach the big circle of our ancestors.

The Gift Of Giving

It is said that if you give, you will get back more than
　you gifted.
Many will argue this, saying "What did they ever do
　for me?"
Many will say, "They never should have gotten into
　this position!"
Many will walk by without even taking notice of the
　less fortunate.

Some might wonder, "What will I get back if I give?"
Some might demand more in return, expecting
　abundance.
Others might appreciate the smile they receive as the
　gift of giving.
What many don't realize is this:
Generous giving is a lesson passed down from our
　ancestors,
Who never expected anything in return.
Giving to others, even just a smile,
Was the way to "keep the circle alive and strong."

Our ancestors never carried anything more than they
　needed.
Today, many hoard; things become possessions.

The elders would ask,
"Why would you give your life for something you
can't take with you?"

Today, the traditions of our ancestors are being
forgotten.
Remember that it isn't what you have that counts,
It's what you do with what you have.

Be thoughtful, as you do not know who your teachers
in this life will be.
Your teacher could be a homeless person,
Gifting you a visual of what your life could be like if
you walked down that dark road.

Be grateful when you gift.
Don't look for a conversation about what they will
do with it.

Sending tobacco prayers out to all: To gift once a day,
even if only by walking away from an argument and
turning your feelings into happiness. You don't know
who is watching you; who will learn how to live from
the model of your actions. A great gift giver teaches
you to keep the circle strong by sharing.

Chakras Are A Relative Of Indigenous Balance

Native wisdom is consistent with the chakra
  teachings.

We indigenous people of Mother Earth believe we are
  all Water Warriors.

Water flows through the creek like energy flows
  through our body.

Our spirit is an energy that keeps our body alive,

Like the chakras are pools of spiraling energy within
  our body.

When life throws things at us that block our
  spiritual growth,

We stop and stand still,

Until a spiritual guide assists with unblocking the flow.

When we open the channels, we open the chakras,

Opening all the rivers within this shell of a body as well.

Mother Earth is our home, our everything while we
  are here.

The Earth chakra is to be found at the base of the spine.

It deals with survival and can be blocked by fear.

What are you most afraid of?

Let your fears become clear to you,

then surrender and release them to open your
   Earth chakra.

Water is very important to Indigenous peoples:

We believe rivers are Mother Earth's veins, which
   keep her alive.

The Water chakra, found between the spine and the
   stomach,

Deals with pleasure, often abused pleasure, and can
   be blocked by guilt.

Look at all the guilt that burdens you.

What do you blame yourself for?

Accept the reality that these things happened,

But do not let them cloud or poison your energy flow.

Guilt is like tainted waters.

If you are to be a positive influence on the world, you
   need to forgive yourself.

The Ojibwe people believe there are eight fires of
   change.

In the chakras, you find fire located in the stomach.

It deals with willpower, and can be blocked by shame.

What are you ashamed of?

What are the biggest disappointments in your life?

To find balance, you have to understand your shame
   and disappointments.

Mother Earth's heartbeat is like the drum.

In the chakras, this is located in the upper chest area.

It deals with love, but is often blocked by grief.

Lay all your grief in front of you.

When you feel a great loss, know that love is a form of energy, swirling all around us.

Identify the pain and then let your love flow into it.

Search your deepest thoughts and feelings.

Let go of old love so that new love can be welcomed.

The ancestors' voices are related to sound.

In the chakras, it's related to the throat.

The throat chakra deals with truth and can be blocked by lies and untruth to oneself.

You cannot lie about yourself; you must accept who you are.

The sparks of your spirit are a reflection of inner Light.

In the chakras, this is found in the center of the forehead.

It deals with insight and can be blocked by illusion,

A misguided distortion of what one perceives as the truth.

The greatest illusion of this world is the illusion of separation.

Things you think are separate and different are
actually the same.

Though we live like we're divided, we are all one
people.

Indigenous people believe in the seven levels of life,
the seven Grandfather teachings.

In the chakra system it is believed that once you open
your seventh chakra,

You can come and go.

We too believe that once we embrace the seven
Grandfather teachings,

Life flows better.

Balance is knowing the Creation Story

And how your spirit lives within this shell we call
the body.

In the chakras, balance is found in the crown of the
head.

It deals with pure cosmic energy and can be blocked
by Earthly attachments.

Once you understand that whatever happens to you
in this world,

Happens to the body and not the spirit,

You can let go of all the garbage and start to live in
balance.

When indigenous people go into a sweatlodge, we meditate in circle and we have a clear understanding of what is important to us: the four elements of this life, fire, water, earth and air.

To master balance you have to learn and practice the seven Grandfather teachings. You must learn to let go of all unnecessary stuff.

The chakra teachings say, open all the chakras and surrender yourself.

We say, think of your attachments and let them go, let the pure cosmic energy flow.

Acts of Kindness

There are going to be those days
When you feel empty, lonely and possibly angry.

We might not notice our behaviors right away,
Until we get into an argument with another
Or come down with a painful headache.

We might act out throughout the day,
Venting and looking for something or someone to
   release this negative energy.

We all have done this in our lifetime, at one time or
   another, and some still do.

But how do we make it stop, where does this come from?

Great-Grandma Margaret would tell me what Little
   Grandma had told her:

"People walk through this life expecting things. When
their demands are not met, they pout, they make
themselves sick. When they get so sick and full of
toxic energy, it has to come out or it will smother
their spirit. They blame everyone else for their own
lack of healthy happiness, becoming mean and taking
it out on everyone."

Sometimes these individuals will do for others

over and over again and later use their giving as ammunition: "I did this and that for them and look what it got me."

You just never know when their negative behavior is going appear.

Great-Grandma Margaret told us what her mother had passed onto her:

"When you see people offering an act of kindness with a price tag stuck to it, don't take it. Stay away from them. Their spirit is sleeping and someone else is dancing in them; they are called "tricksters." They will be your best teachers while you are here on Mother Earth. Learn who they are and pray for them; pray really hard for them."

She told us that these individuals will wake their spirits and when they come clear to life, they will still carry this sickness with them. Their sickness will come and go as their spirit becomes stronger, they will have to master their strength to banish this trickster.

She continued, "If you feed this trickster by continuing the negative energy, talking bad about them or even fighting with them, they will sneak into

you and put your spirit to sleep. Watch out for them,"
she said.

These are lessons I teach my children so they will
know their teachers and they will know how to
maintain their strength. I pass on this story to you
all as I pray with tobacco thoughts to all to be strong,
wake your spirit, be kind to yourself by knowing your
surroundings and don't blame others, just pray for
them, pray really hard for them to awake.

Life is good; remember to share your medicine smiles.

Positive Energy From A Negative Source

Anger is only the icing on the cake
That patiently awaits the explosion
Of the ingredients that it was formed from.

When you meet an angry person, don't judge them
    for their shortcomings.
See the beauty in the energy that radiates from them.

You say, "What? Are you crazy? I stay away from
    people like that!"

Be the student that sees beyond this world's views.
See the spiritual energy that flows from one person
    to another.
It's how you use this energy that determines your own
    intelligence.

Think about it; when someone makes you mad, or
when someone makes you feel fearful, think about the
energy that flows restlessly throughout your body.
You can either embrace the anger and respond in kind,
Or you can take this energy and walk away.

You can use this energy to finish a project that you
    have been putting off for a long time,

Or you can go for a walk and think about life.

Visualize your life like a drawing board,
Color your happiness in and then use this energy to
seek it out.

The question to ask of angry situations is:
What were you doing when you met this situation?
What place in your life were you in?

Creator and our ancestors are around us, bringing gifts,
Sometimes in the form of messages that awaken us in
the form of anger.
Find your balance in this teaching and move
forward.

Never judge the deliverer of anger.
Just say prayers for them of thankfulness that they
gifted you this energy.
When you walk away without responding to them,
you gift them a life lesson.

Life is good today; enjoy being a student of life.

You Are Not The Judge; You Are The Student

We cannot tell our fellow brothers and sisters how to
   live their lives,
Though we often think we can.

We do not know what journey took them down this path,
But we often assume the worst.

We should not act like we live a better life than theirs,
But we often do.

We should not glamorize our lives and compare
   ourselves to others,
But it happens more than we think.

When you find yourself looking at a less fortunate
   person—
A homeless person, a drunk, a druggy person who
   walks in dark places;
When you find yourself thinking they are worthless;
When you find yourself fearful of them;
When you find yourself judging their lives;
Think this thought:
Creator put all kinds of spirits on Mother Earth to
   interact with one another
In a circle of communication.

When you find yourselves judging another,
Do not see them as less than you.
Thank them for showing you that this could have
   been your path.

Today, our children have lost the understanding
Of how to live a friendly good life, as our ancestors
   taught us.

We do not know what the Creator has in store for us
   until we trust in the "We."

We can help our fellow brothers and sisters by
   offering a medicine smile.
We can offer some change, some food, some kindness
   without judgment.
We can support the doorways that offer a lifetime
   commitment to healing.

We can be thankful that we chose to walk in kindness,
   gentleness and health here on Mother Earth.

We can be thankful for our teachers who remind us
   that there is a dark world waiting for each of us if
   we do not stand in balance with creation.

Each person's body is like a television, replaying life's journeys over and over again.

Your spirit is the energy plug that fits into the wall of life's tomorrows.

You can keep your life in replay and be reminded of your shortcomings by witnessing others,

Or you can unplug and let your spiritual energy take you to the places of happiness intended for you.

Today is a gift, a new day to live.

Sending tobacco prayers out to all people and animals, Creators' creations, for strength and healing, to remind themselves that this life is a classroom of equality and balance.

Today is a good day to breathe. Today is a good day.

Happiness Is A Choice

Happiness is natural, if you have made the journey
  yourself.

If you choose to ride on the shirttails of others to
  make you happy,

Be prepared for all their disappointments as well.

If you choose to get off their journey and start
  your own,

Be prepared for excitement that only you can bank in
  your memory—

It's yours, all yours.

If you choose to cross that line of should I, could I, or
  how can I,

Just know you have all your ancestors inside you,
  fighting for you to do it.

If you choose not to do it and continue your path of
  expecting others to make you happy,

Just know that you and you alone closed the
  ancestors' doorway.

They are holding it open for you,

Sending you the strength to be as happy as they intended you to be.

Sending tobacco prayers to all who fight loneliness, isolation and low self-esteem.

Remember, you were not born this way! This is a learned emotion; you can choose to be the student of these lessons or you can walk away from this classroom of craziness and become the teacher of "I did it and so can you," leading by smiling.

Life is good today and we are open to all the happiness that we meet.

The Gift Of A Day

It's a good day to walk Mother Earth.

We are gifted 24 hours of awesomeness.

We are gifted with 1,440 minutes of adventure
hunting.

We are gifted with 86,400 seconds of life
opportunities.

We are gifted this each day.

As we unwrap each day, we determine its beauty.

Some may say:

I hate living.

No one cares about me.

Life is hard.

*I never knew true love or the abundance of a loving
family.*

Some may feel:

I love my life.

It feels good to be needed.

Life is an adventure.

*Family is everything and the joy is within our
relationships.*

Some may abuse the feelings of others, saying:

I can have as many relationships as I want.

I can have many children with different people.

I can do as I please; no one is going to tell me what to do.

I am my own person and they will do as I want.

Some may smile and say:

I am grateful for this day to be with my loved ones.

I am blessed that I can share true happiness with another.

I am excited to teach a little one joy.

I am overwhelmed that I have been gifted another day to walk on Mother Earth.

We are the givers and receivers of life's journeys.

We create our own foundations.

We create our own happiness, as well as our own miseries.

We are the only designers of our destiny.

Life will shine when we take back the powers that we chose to throw away.

Life can be turned around.

Life is a choice, so choose wisely.

Life is a unique opportunity.

It's never too late to start a new chapter of life.

It's never too late to say, "One day at a time," or "One moment at a time."

It's never too early to begin to feel joy.

Every day you have the choice of being early or a bit late. At least you made it.

It's a good day to embrace life and walk away from a dark path.

Sending tobacco prayers out to all, to challenge yourself to be the treasure, the beautiful gift that Creator knows you to be. Life is good and it is a good day to walk on the beautiful Mother we call Earth and to breathe in Father Sky's breath.

It's a good day.

Spiritual Drumbeat

Be reminded of what keeps your heart beating.
Be reminded that you are not alone.

Be reminded that you can hear a daily rhythm.

Be reminded that you carry only what you choose to
pick up.

Spiritual strength comes from your ancestors, who
breathe inside your every cell.

Your breath is a whisper of your ancestors.

Your reflection is of the ones that came before you.

Your weakness is your cry for your ancestors' approval.

To open your eyes or insight to this world we call
Mother Earth

Is like soaring through the Universe with spirit sparks.

To feel is to receive a message of guidance, no matter
the journey.

To listen to all the messages that you encounter

Is like journeying through the halls of life's
instructions.

To believe is to trust that you have made your ancestors proud—

By remembering their teachings, they will not be forgotten.

Your spirit keeps your heartbeat in rhythm.

When it beats fast, you are in trouble,

When it beats slow, you are in trouble.

You must find balance in the rhythm to live a journey of spiritual connection,

Living the "We" and not the me.

This spiritual heartbeat belongs to you and all your ancestors who made your journey possible.

Sending tobacco prayers out to all who are off their rhythm, to remind them that life is as good as they want it to be and to take ownership of their pathway here on Mother Earth.

Smile, it is powerful medicine.

Life is good today.

My daughters Fonda and Francisca (holding her youngest son DJ) at a March on Pipelines and Clean Water in St. Paul, Minnesota, Spring 2017. I was asked to be one of the main speakers and give a prayer before the March. Also pictured is my daughters' half sister Hannah, who I adore; she is from their father's last marriage, and I share a special relationship with her.

IV. PRAYERS
IN MOTION

Free Will

As I stand at the threshold of life,

How do I see my worth?

How do I determine my worldly contribution?

How do I embrace my spirit?

As a child, I was presented with my life's challenges.

As a young person, I confused my path with these
challenges.

As an adult, I embraced the mess.

As an Elder, I looked back at my life and I knew I
had free will.

I am the author of my life,

I am the artist who will draw the beauty of today,

I am a person who understands free will.

If I accept the things I cannot change,

I understand I can change the things that are
important to me.

Serenity is what I make of my life.

Creator, grant me the understanding of free will today!

The Journey

There was a time when I felt worthless.
There was a time when I felt hopeless.
There was a time when my world was dark.
There was a time when I did not want to go on.

Why was I allowed to enter this dark world?
Where was all the happiness when I entered this world?
When did the lights go out?
Who paved this rugged path for me?

I look towards Mother Earth and ask her to embrace me,
But her winds tell me no.
I look to Father Sky and ask him to please help me
    soar home,
But he gently tells me no.

I have never felt so lost.
I have no one to turn to as they have all turned from me.
I close my eyes tightly and soar towards my inner spirit.
I see myself wanting to awaken,
But something is there that keeps me asleep.

As I lie sleeping, I suddenly find myself leaving my shell.

I feel fear and, at the same time, I feel free.

In the distance, I see my grandmothers smiling.

They take me on a journey and remind me of a time
yet to come.

I awaken full of a feeling like no other.

I feel eager, I feel strong, I feel powerful!

I close my eyes for a moment to thank my
grandmothers for this gift.

I promise them I will do my best as I see their light.

I am a great-granddaughter,

I am a granddaughter, I am a daughter.

I am from them, I am free—

I am a Red Road Warrior woman—I am me!

Faith

If you keep looking for guidance in the same direction
You were looking while you were using,
You are seeking failure!

If you trust in yourself to watch over the inner spirit
That lies sleeping inside of you,
Then you are ready to wake and live another path.

What you have to be reminded of
Is that you are much stronger than you think.
There has always been this Warrior Woman in you,
Watching over your inner spirit.

You have to embrace yourself
And accept that you are this Warrior Woman,
You are this sleeping spirit, now ready to wake up.

You have been taught to accept all the negatives and
   shortcomings of life,

And to continue to fuel your surroundings with these
  teachings.

STOP IT!

You have a choice in this short life:

To either keep making yourself miserable

Or to be happy.

You pick the path.

It's not that scary to let go of all the garbage.

So, DO IT!

Look back at yesterday,

Give yourself time,

Give yourself permission to mourn

As you let go of all the pain that someone gave you

Or what you did to yourself.

Then, LET IT GO!

It was scary to take that first step when you were a baby,

But there was someone to catch you.

Now, fast forward to today,

As you take that first step onto the Red Road,

Just know that there will be many of us to help catch you if you fall.

We are called "Faith Deliverers" and we just delivered your first dose of faith to help you take this step.

Tobacco prayers go out to all who keep taking that first step over and over. Just know that these are "Faith Wisdom Lessons." Once you get it, you will have to pass on your extra FAITH to others who are in need of it.

Life is good today.

The Journey From Within

Our creation story speaks of our togetherness
throughout time here on Mother Earth.

Our spirit soared into this blanket of a body it lives
in, thus we live together, spirit and body living in
the "We."

Life is like a written book.

Each chapter is made up of many adventures,
featuring many emotions.

Sometimes we get stuck with a chapter that keeps
repeating itself.

Life is like a tapestry.

Each color is a heartfelt event; each stitch is like a
wound one experienced.

Often the tapestry will display all the craziness of the
adventures one has lived.

Life is like music.

Each rhythm shows the anger or the happiness that
one experienced.

Each word within the song expresses happiness or sorrow.

Often, this will be the calling card for the next dance
in life.

Remember this:

You are the author of the book of your life.

You can change anything within your chapters.

Most of all, be sure your last chapter is a happy one.

You are the seamstress, the tailor, the designer of your
 tapestry.

You can always add beauty and understanding,
 stitching in your truth.

You are the musician, the songwriter of the tune you
 dance to.

You can always end everything on a good note.

Sending tobacco prayers out to all: To know that you
carry the key to opening your inner happiness; you
just have to allow your inner spirit to awaken and
stay awake.

Life is good today.

The True Gift

Today, our expectations are just that:
Things we expect, we demand!
What if something happens that reminds each of us
What the true gift is?

What if someone changes our expectations suddenly?
What if the life we normally live isn't there any longer?
What if we are told there is no future as we know it?

Can you ever remember an Elder teaching you the
  value of life?

Can you remember your life shifting?

Can you remember wanting a life that was in the past?

Can you remember the feeling of true love that
  has faded?

Take a moment, STOP right where you are now;

Close your eyes and think about the happiest moment
  in your life.

Write down the year it was.

The moment you open your eyes in the morning,

Breathe in, remembering that this breath comes from
   your ancestors.

Feel everything that is touching your body

And give thanks for keeping you rested and safe the
   night before.

Then, as you take your first drink of water,

Be thankful as it waters your plant of a body.

Feel the nourishment as you splash the water on
   your face.

Take a moment to realize that you have the freedom
   to let your mind wander.

When you do these daily appreciation exercises,

Make a list of four things you want.

Paint them in your mind, body and spirit

And tell yourself you are worthy.

Life is the true gift.

How you take care of yourself determines the rewards.

Self-worth is the vault that waits to be filled.

Fire....the warmth within you.

Air...the breath of your ancestors that live within you.

Water...the purest flow that keeps your plant of a body alive to house your spirit.

Mother Earth...she provides an abundance of nourishment for you.

Life is as good as you make it.

The teacher, the guide, the strength rests within each of you.

When you feel alone, be reminded that there are two of you,

Your body and your spirit,

Along with the breath of your ancestors.

Sending tobacco prayers out to all to be reminded that there is a warrior within each of you and there is a greener pasture waiting for you to enter.

Don't Forget To Water Your Plant

"If we do not nourish ourselves on the lessons of
life, listening to our ancestors' stories, giving time for
Creator, building a genuine relationship with all that
is good, then we are going to dry up."

Each person has their own journey to walk on.
On this journey, there are many crossroads.
Curiosity may steer you into challenges that will take
   you off the good path.
Darkness on your journey will make you realize you
   were brighter than you thought.

Our lessons of wonder will remind each of us of our
   inner strengths.
Our lessons of doubt will restore hope.
Our lessons of desire will become real.
Our lessons of balance will teach us the full
   understanding of right and wrong.

Our grandfathers used to say "be careful what you
   wish for."
Our grandmothers used to say "dream big."
Our ancestors told their stories.

Struggling with our behavior on our journey shows us
   the wisdom of these teachings.

These teachings are everywhere; we will always be
reminded of them.

When we feel at our lowest, there will be tears.
These tears are reminders that our body is a plant that
houses our tired spirit.
We can gift ourselves the freedom to bring ourselves
back to life.

Sending tobacco prayers out to all:

When you look at, touch or taste water; when you feel
like your beauty is no longer; when you feel lifeless,
empty and lost; be reminded that you are your own
water carriers.

You have the ability to water the plant of life and
bring back the beauty and life of the plant you call
your body. The strength lives within you—awaken your
power, awaken your spirit.

Life is good today, be thankful for your tears as they
are the gift of water.

Finding A Common Spiritual Ground

It's a chaotic world out there.

So many messages...

So many beliefs...

So many doors to open.

Searching to find yourself involves a journey to the unknown.

Who do you believe is giving you the right life instructions?

How will we know the lesson is being given by the correct teacher?

Why is life so challenging?

To awaken within yourself is the most fearful challenge of all.

To be open to your own inner knowledge will be an awakening.

Knowing who you are will determine your growth.

To acknowledge your strength from within will be overwhelming.

You will find yourself attracted to strong spiritual people

Who walk silently on Mother Earth.

You will feel the hunger to fill yourself with the unknown.

You will surrender to your own energy.

You will look for guidance and will find it within yourself.

Life will begin to seem awesome.

People around you will start to feel different to you.

The earth will become a landscape of adventures.

Your feet will be eager to start many new journeys.

You will realize that the common ground you were searching for was already inside you.

As your spiritual energy awakened, your ancestors' teachings spoke to you.

Your strength came from the burst of energy that fueled the journey

That has been patiently awaiting you all along.

Your body met your spirit and learned that there are two of you, the "We."

You have a partner; you are not alone.

You have a choice in the lessons you will learn.

Your common ground has been underneath your feet

Since the day you entered this world we call
  Mother Earth.

Now, run with the wind,

Glide with the wings of an eagle

And soar on the breath of your ancestors.

Sending tobacco prayers out to all: Remember,
everything you seek is within you, everything you
admire in others, lives within you. So water your body
and watch your spirit grow.

Life is good today.

To Stand Within Your Own Spirituality

There will come a day when something or someone

Will entice you with their overview of what they think
you need.

It may happen when you are a child.

It may happen when you are a young adult.

It may happen when you think you are an adult.

It might even happen when you are an elder.

These voices will express what was taught to them,
saying,

"Do as I do, say as I say."

There will come a time when you become angry,
nervous, and unsure in your gut.

Then, it will happen:

An inner voice will question these moments.

An overwhelming feeling will trigger a concern.

Your body will feel a chill of uncertainty.

Your spirit will rise up inside you and say STOP—
let's think about this one.

When your spirit awakens, look out,

As you will begin to stand strong on your two feet.

Your senses will awaken,

As these are your ancestors within you,

Guiding you through the storm of deceit.

When your emotions take over,

This is the time to bring yourself back into balance.

A spiritual awakening is taking place, a maturity of
peace is happening.

Life will take on new meaning.

A clear presence of reality will appear.

Your warrior wings will lift you up.

You will stand with your own spirituality,

And this will start to feel familiar,

As this is what was intended for you since you entered Mother Earth.

Life is good as long as you take ownership of your own journey and walk the good life.

Sending tobacco prayers out to all: To believe in yourselves and stop following false leaders that lead you down dark roads. Be reminded that it has always been about CHOICE and freewill. Take back your power and start living the good life of the Red Road.

Life Breeds Warriors

Life presents challenges.

When you run from them, they will catch up to you.

What you have to remember is this:

When the challenges catch you, they will find you
weak and more vulnerable.

What you will be afraid of is yourself:

Am I able to face this and conquer what is put
before my path?

Time has a beginning and it also has an end for the
blanket of a body.

Eternity whispers in the wind that the spirit will
last forever.

My father would tell us that it's what we do with
our challenges

That builds our character;

There is no one else to blame for our own
shortcomings.

We can either embrace our weaknesses

Or pass on the courage that we have earned.

My grandfather would say that if life put a challenge before you,

Creator knew the Warrior in you.

Our grandmothers would smile from a distance,

Knowing that lessons about exterior strength had to be told by a male figure.

They also said that spiritual strength came from both male and female

And in time, many would forget this if they failed to be challenged to be a Life's Warrior.

Sending out tobacco prayers to all: To know the Warrior Spirit within you. Today is a good day as we meet our weaknesses with our spiritual strength.

There Is A Reason We Are Called Warriors

Creator never let go of my hands,
When I so desperately wanted to not be here.

Creator delivers the whispers of strength
That were given to our ancestors in hard times,
Along with breezes of warmth in happy times.

Creator is called a deliverer for a reason;
We believe that the special delivery package is you.

Creator stands strong with extending arms
That reach clear across this planet we call home.
This strength is equally gifted to every living thing
That breathes the breath of Mother Earth.

The goodness of creation is within you,
Or Creator would have never provided you with
    this body,
So your spirit can rest in it while here on Mother Earth.

The instructions of living, Creator left up to you.

You can choose what your mind thinks.

You can choose what actions you take.

You can choose to teach good or bad.

You can choose to be all you can be.

The past sounds within each of us, waves of music
called Ancestors.

The ancestors taught us that the only war that goes on
is the one inside you,

When you are off balance.

Your body will argue with your spirit about what is
right or wrong.

The greatest war of all, will be when your body
overcomes your spirit

And you join in on the dark path here on Mother
Earth.

These are called man-made wars.

The spirit that rests inside of you will be put to sleep,

The balance of life will falter.

Only when you realize the loneliness within you,

Will you remember that the you can restore balance by awakening your spirit.

Then the light of goodness will come on.

Beauty will appear everywhere when balance is restored.

Remember, the enemy always lurks in dark places with enticing temptations,

The trickster waiting for your return.

The war will end when you know your strengths and walk in balance.

Sending tobacco prayers out to all who feel they are lonely, weak and disrupted. Within these prayers rests a reminder that you are not alone, defeated or confused. You have just fallen out of balance and you forgot that your ancestors rest within you. All you have to do is awaken the spirit within you and wait for the beauty to return. The awakening is the end of war for you.

Life is good today.

Tobacco Prayers In Motion

Praying is not done when you are in trouble.

Praying is not about asking for more than you need.

Praying is not begging for change in a moment of crisis.

Praying is not about asking for help for others' shortcomings.

Prayers are meant to have movement.

Prayer gives you strength to help your fellow human beings,

Offering a way to turn on the light of hope.

To pray is to honor living a healthy life,

To show others that your shell of a body needs to be cared for,

So your spirit can continue on.

To pray is to ask for patience,

To rethink your reactions, to avoid responding in anger.

To pray is to ask for balance within yourself,

To remind yourself not to caretake others when your
own space is toxic;

Take care of yourself first.

Prayer in motion is walking a positive pathway.

Prayer in motion is taking care of your personal space.

Prayer in motion is stepping forward positively
after a crisis.

Prayer in motion is taking positive actions for yourself

Without depending on others to do your wishes.

Prayers are heard.

Each time you ask for something,

Be reminded that your ancestors live within you.

Their DNA exists within your shell of a body.

Our spirit soars within our body.

Once we leave Mother Earth and join the Grand
Circle of Life,

We will come face to face with our ancestors.

What type of conversations will you have?

Sending tobacco prayers out to all, to live within your own journey prayers. Do unto others in a positive way, no matter what.

Life is good today.

The Gathering

We woke today
To a world that is not prepared
For the awakening of more than a thousand
   strong women.

We breathe the scent of wild flowers
As we whisper to the grandparents before us:

*We are here, we have awoken. We will take these lessons
that you have taught us throughout time and share them,
along with the blessings of the Red Road.*

We are grateful for all the Nations gathering here.

*We give thanks to all the directions for balancing our
pure thoughts to undo the damage that has contaminated
us as a Nation.*

*We will humble ourselves to others and stay on equal
ground with them until they can soar with you, Great
Creator.*

*We are alive, we are strong, we are Warrior Women who
   have awoken.*

Ancestral Pride: A Partnership with the Past

We have become a checklist of requirements.
We have become a list of dismissals.
We have become someone else's option.
We have become someone else's imagination.

We cannot lose memory, if it was never introduced.
But what we can remember is that we exist because we
   are descendants.
Even if they removed us from our people,
We can feel our ancestral spirit, which soars within
   our bodies.

To exist as our ancestors wish for us,
We need to remember the many storms they have
   survived,
The many wars they have fought,
The many miles they have walked,
The medicines they treasured,
The land they cared for.

For I am of the "WE."
My body and spirit are one.
My relatives who have passed on,
Still live within me.

My children reflect our past,
My life matters, because my ancestors are real.

What matters are the elements that were gifted to
   each of us:
Water, to keep this plant of a body alive,
Fire, to keep this body warm,
Air, to keep this body breathing healthy,
Earth, to keep this body nourished,
So that our spirit may exist within this world.

Sending tobacco prayers out to all to STOP believing
that material things will make you happy. It's okay to
have as long as you remind yourself that it's not the
end of the world if you don't have. Give yourself a
moment to relax and remember your ancestors, who
journeyed through the storms to make sure you had
a happy tomorrow. They continue to exist. As long as
our ancestors are smiling at what we are doing today,
we are making them proud.

Eagle Dreams

An Elder man spoke of his disappointments about
   Native events these days.

In his conversation he spoke of people "staggering
down paths to nowhere other than to the bank to
deposit their checks from serving on our Tribal
Councils."

You could feel his sorrow as he spoke of the problems
   of his people.

As we looked around, we did not see a dry eye in
   the circle.

After this man sat down, an Elder woman stood up to
   speak and told of her dreams:

*There were four Eagles soaring around my house every day
   and then on the seventh day one flew off.*

*The three Eagles continued to soar around for another
   seven days and then one flew off.*

*The remaining two Eagles were getting tired, very tired,
   but they continued to soar until the seventh day came and
   one flew off.*

As I watched the one Eagle soaring, the Elder woman said, I noticed that there was a crowd of young people looking up at the skies and all were wondering the same thing l was: where did the other Eagles go and how can I help this one who is left?

As the seventh day came near, four Grandmothers appeared. They held their arms out and the remaining Eagle swooped down and rested on one of the Grandmothers' shoulders.

The other three Grandmothers opened their shawls and out flew three Eagles, who soared out, then swooped down and rested on the other three Grandmothers' shoulders.

The tired Eagle that flew for 28 days straight spread his wings and turned into a very old man.

Turning around to speak to the audience, which had grown very large, he said:

"The Eagles are your pathways to find us. When you ignore their needs, you close the doorway to our existence." Then he turned back into an Eagle and soared off to the North. One by one the Eagles flew into all four directions.

The four Grandmothers smiled and one spoke softly in her language, which all could understand. She said: "Our spirits are getting dim; we have used our last light *to guide you. If the young ones do not know our ways, the light will go out for good and you will not find us."*

Then, one by one, each Grandmother walked into the four directions and faded away.

This Elder woman said, "I know I am not the only one having these dreams, but they also told me that they whisper the teachings and no one is listening anymore."

She sat down and as we looked around, again there was not a dry eye in the circle.

As our Ancestors have spoken of, there is an awakening happening.

It is up to us Elders to remind the young of our grandparents' stories.

When our Tribal Council needs a leader and all these people come out of the woodwork wanting my vote, I ask them this question: "What have you done for our people without getting a paycheck for it?"

Legacy is this:

It's not the voice of change that carries our existence towards the future,

It's the actions of those who do not seek notice for
  their goodwill.
They are there, you just have to look for them and
  seek out the good medicine of their smiles.
We all know who they are in our communities; they
  are few, but they are there.

This seventh generation is going to be our greatest test
to survive as a people, as a Nation. But we Elders hear
and feel the awakenings.

Sending tobacco prayers out to all to awake.

A Spirit's Prayer

I rest my spirit on the wings of Brother Eagle,
Enjoying the gentle breezes of Father Sky's breath.

As we soar to the corners of Mother Earth,
I watch the pathways of my life pass by,
And I see my loved ones feeling great sorrow.

I ask Brother Eagle to soar low so I may send thoughts
of goodwill.
I ask the Creator to please lessen their pain,
To please let them know I am okay,
To let them know I am excited about entering the
great circle,
That I will tell our relatives of the journeys I have taken.

I am ready to go home.
I witnessed today that I was loved,
That I leave a legacy,
That I will not be forgotten.

As Brother Eagle takes me on my last soar,
I hear all the other Brother and Sister Eagles singing,
Telling me their joyful song will be heard.

I see my relatives welcoming me into the divine circle.
I am not alone, for I am home.

Walking the Red Road... With Gratitude for my Family, Friends and Teachers

I'm a blessed person, who has lived a very interesting life with many memories that make me laugh, cry and scream for more. The many chapters in my life are filled with adventure, thrills and chaos, but most of all with joy!

I have been blessed with many relatives, extended relatives and adopted relatives who have filled every corner of my thoughts and my heart. I could not have moved forward into the Love and Light if it weren't for the ones who kept continuously turning on these lights.

And then there are many other teachers—the ones who my father told me would be my best teachers in life, the people that you don't want to be like; their mistakes would teach you not to follow in their footsteps!

I try to be as traditional as my elders have taught me to be. My father was my rock; he taught me everything from making my bed first thing in the morning to saying my prayers at night. There was never a dull moment with him. I would drink black coffee while doing my chores as he told me stories from his life and all the lessons that his relatives taught him.

My mother Ruby was a gem to many but in my earlier days, I didn't feel this. It wasn't until I was older that I understood why she treated me and my sisters the way she did. When I understood what she went through in her early years, I realized it was her way of trying to make us stronger than she had been. I never had a chance to tell her I loved her when she was alive, but I think she knew I how much I craved this sharing. Today, I can sing her name and tell the Heavens, the grand circle of life, how much I love her. I can't wait to hug her and tell her in person when I walk on.

I wouldn't be a complete person if it weren't for my siblings:

- Mary Sr., who I never met; I was named after her as she died at a very early age.

- My brother Eddie, who I thought of as my second Dad. My brother Eddie was handicapped and a medicine man with knowledge beyond the Stars and Heavens; he was a child of the Universe and Stars. Even though he never was married or had children, he left behind many children who wished he was their father as he gifted so many with compassion and unconditional love—from his sharing of community soup bowls for hungry people, to medicines from Mother Earth.

- Walter, who we called Wally, also never had children; he spent the majority of his life in prison for a community crime, though it was later discovered that he didn't do what he had been convicted of. Spending more than 30 years in prison held him in that frame of fear when he got out; he could never just be happy and secure. But I can tell you this, he was a great brother and uncle.

- Then there was my older sister Lilly, who I didn't get to know until later in life, as I held it against her for leaving me when they removed her from our home. She had been like my mother. She too experienced a hard life with alcohol, but later in life she stood on her own two feet and gave everything to her younger daughter and her grandchildren. My older sister taught me compassion and to remember not to judge another as we don't know their truth. She was the best and I wish every day that I had made more time for her when she was alive.

- My brother Loren, "Butch," had one biological son and two stepchildren who he treated as his own. He too had a difficult life and it wasn't until later in life that he sobered up and took responsibility for being a good Dad. He suffered badly as a diabetic, including loss of eyesight and living on daily dialysis. My brother, like my father, was a strong man with guidance from the ancestors.

- My other brother, Charles Junior, had his demons from our earlier years from being taken away from our parents. He was put into the military right out of jail at the age of 15. He faced the Vietnam war and all the nightmares from then on, so he never got a chance to heal. I think the only time I saw him smile, with such great love, is when he had his children and then his grandchildren. He gave his best but the best wasn't enough; he just couldn't free himself from all the demons that kept him from happiness. He died a tragic death, leaving behind three daughters and one son who met his own death soon after his father died.

- Shortly after my birth my mother gave birth to another son by the name of John. He was like my twin, as this brother could never do anything wrong in my eyes. When he was younger he had medical problems and was very special to me. Of all my brothers, he is the one who looks just like our father. He has two sons and grandchildren whom he adores.

- After him came my little brother Lenny. He married and had a son and daughter, and then his life was cut short, just like that! He was the comedian of the family and the peskiest one of all and we miss him every moment of the day. He left behind a beautiful family who had to learn the difficult lessons of life on their own and become the strong adults they are today.

- We have a brother by the name of Randall, who was one of the first children to be shown on television for adoption. He was taken from my mother when she lived in Minneapolis due to her absence and drinking. He was not returned to my father because the welfare thought my father was too old to care for him and my other younger brother and sister. To this very day we celebrate his birthday and wonder if he ever knew that we looked for him and that he was never forgotten. Randy needs to know that there was always an empty chair at the table of our family celebrations; he was never forgotten, he was loved from afar.

- My younger sister Cathy was named after our mother and we called her "Kitty Kat." She lived a very brief life here on Mother Earth as she was murdered, leaving behind three beautiful boys. I think she always knew her life here was going to be short. She lived hard and always carried the memory of our mother, as she and my baby brother Darrell, who we called "Odie," were there with our mother when she died. Cathy, who was three years old at the time, could never lay to rest her grief at our mother's passing. What happened with her thoughts in those two days of being with our deceased mother brought dimness to her life.

From the time that our neighbor came over to discover the death, to when we finally buried our mother, was like a thousand lifetimes for her. No one talked to her about these feelings when she went into her first treatment center for addiction. Anger often became her way out, all the way up to her untimely death. Towards the end, she too changed her life around as if she knew her time here was limited. She too wanted to come home to the reservation and never leave again. One thing about her is that she loved her boys unconditionally.

- My younger brother was too little to remember our mother's death, but carried an emptiness within him. Darrell went on to have a family with two beautiful biological children and he also adopted two handsome young boys (whom he considers his biological sons). He divorced but continues to have a friendly relationship with their mother.

- Then it comes to the very last sibling. When my mother passed she was carrying our sibling and was nearly full term. Our sibling rests with our mother in our family plot in the Bena cemetery, which my father visited every day after her death. Now my parents are together again along with ten of my siblings, as besides me only John and Darrell are left here on Mother Earth.

My daughters Francisca and Fonda at their 2016 graduation from St. Catherine's University in St. Paul, Minnesota. This photo is from my collection of "Angel Faces," which I think my daughters started when they were very little and got into trouble. We celebrate our children's victories, as many of the Free World still believe that the majority of Indigenous people are uneducated. Plus, at one time these two women were raising their children alone and were climbing mountains that many thought they could not surmount.

My greatest teachers in life have been my children and their children and I would like to express my love and gratitude to them here.

- My daughter Fonda is not only my helper on my path but also my eldest child. You always have a special place in your heart for your first-born and this is true for our relationship. She taught me a lot in her first five years, before her sister was born; we developed a friendship and she taught me how to get over my fear of my parenting skills. I was worried that I would I repeat my mother's actions. This was a constant struggle, as I wanted my first-born to feel unconditional love. I didn't realize that she received these feelings of trust from me until later in life. She helped bring back to me the first memories I had of my family, before our foundation was interrupted. I believe we are on the right path as I witness her loving care of her children and her nurturing of her siblings and nieces and nephews, and especially her granddaughter. She has blessed me with three beautiful grandchildren, Keely, Aki and Lilly. Then my eldest granddaughter Keely blessed me with my first great-granddaughter, Manidoo, who makes me laugh every day and keeps me honest.

- Francisca, my youngest daughter, is a joy to me as well; she is the strength in keeping our family traditions going, from family picnics to birthday parties and holiday parties. She blessed me

with five beautiful grandchildren, who are all so
talented within our culture and traditions. My
grandson Mah-Koonce Inni not only overcame
a birth defect that could have taken his life,
he has turned into a strong young man who
is very accomplished in music. Ruby is named
after my mother and she is a strong woman
who has faced many challenges in life, but never
forgets to remind herself she overcame many
and is a Warrior Woman herself. Ruby is also a
traditional helper of mine, and has a beautiful
singing voice. Zyra, her younger sister, is also
talented within our Ojibwe traditions and dances,
as well as in beading and painting. Then we have
the baby girl Ava—she is a gem who makes me
smile from ear to ear with her silliness. And of
course we cannot forget about baby DJ, who, since
he was born, has been to just as many rallies and
protests as I have. This family has been blessed
with a newcomer to the family, Dory, Francisca's
husband. He willingly took the responsibilities of
being a father to all and is a great family man who
provides well for them all.

Joshua, Ozzie and Jedidiah are my younger sister
Cathy's sons, who I raised as my own after her murder
in 1989. These young men have had to struggle
through life's wars in the aftermath of their mother's
death, trying to heal from her absence. They have
taught me so much about parenting and being a
friend with patience.

- Joshua remains single with high interests of starting another chapter of life by moving away from home.

- Ozzie is my constant reminder that I have more to learn, and that I need to have patience and just be there for him when he needs me. This young man breaks barriers; I believe his daughter Amaya Jane helped him with this. He also has another son that I wish we could know more about and create memories with.

- Jedidiah is the middle chapter of my teachings on parenting, by which I mean, you know how sometimes you get stuck in a book and you have to re-read chapters just to get the essence of the teaching? Well this is Jed: just when I think I know him, something turns ups and surprises me. Jed has two beautiful young sons, Wyat and Tucker. These two boys have been a mirror for my parenting of their father. When Jed is hyper, these little ones are the medicine that calms him.

Then we have my four younger sons:

- William Wade, who we are always trying to marry off as he is so giving, funny and honest in his relationships. Yes, I said relationships; he just needs to commit to marriage and know that this is not a bad word or avenue.

- Christian is my son who carries the weight of pain

and just keeps on trying to do his best. Every time I think of him, tears flow, as this young man just doesn't know how much I really love him.

- Just when my tears flow, my two youngest boys Jonathan and Chauncey brighten up life for me. These two young men have medical conditions that they overcome daily. With the help of many, Jonathan has overcome many obstacles and depressions and he continues to shine in trying to manage on his own in life.

- My youngest, Chauncey, is my gifted and medically fragile son who is the glue that holds our entire family together. I brought him home from the hospital in a hospice setting, but I just knew that it was not his time to depart from this life. He was born with many medical conditions and heart problems that came from living in an unhealthy womb. His biological mother was a dear woman with some demons that just overtook her world; she passed away from alcohol poisoning. I can never speak ill of this woman, as she struggled with so much; I know that given the chance in life, she would have been a beautiful woman. Every day, when I hug Chauncey, I whisper to her in the heavens that I am hugging him for her.

In Indigenous cultures, we have extended relatives and treat them as if they were siblings. My mother's brothers and sisters and their children are all like my brothers and sisters; we are all very close. One relative who I think of especially as my sister is Carol June White-Sargent-Buckanaga-Fairbanks. She was the closest to me of all my cousins and was like another mother to me. I could go on and on about all my relatives and how much I cherish them all; I could write a series of books about our lives but choose to end here.

I also have other very special sister friends: Barbara Denny, Sharyl WhiteHawk, Linda Woods, Jackie Sam, Devi Tide and the Grandmothers, along with so many others.

When I got divorced, I got to keep one thing and that was my mother-in-law, Margaret "Muggins" Smith, who was the best: my teacher, my mother, my best friend.

I am a blessed person and Creator has always been looking out for me. Creator only gave me what he/she knew I could handle. I just recently embraced the fact that I have never been alone: my ancestors are not only within me, they stand behind and around me. I am blessed; and I am loved; and I love sharing the gifts that were given to me. I do my best to be nice to everyone because life is short.

Life is good. Today is a good day to be alive and healthy, and to thank all the beautiful children and people in my life who call me Mom, Grandmother/Kookum, Aunty and sister.

Tobacco Prayer to the World

Never forget the beginning, never forget your
ancestors' journeys here on Mother Earth, never
forget about your Creator. When you forget about
everything, you lose yourself to the world of
disparities and invite all that comes with it. You
surrender to a weakness that was never gifted to you.

You see, we are made up of the four elements.
Everything on Mother Earth is made of the four
elements, and we are all related through this
connection. The gift of breath, the gift of warmth, the
gift of nourishment and the gift of water—this is who
we all are. We are gifts from the Creator; we are his/
her creations and students while we are here. We are
of the Oneness.

It was man who forgot this first teaching and
started dividing up life, not Creator. Creator did
not invent prejudice or hate. Creator's belief in each
of us was strong, as he/she knew that we could learn
from every lesson that was laid before us, overcome
our challenges and move forward. If it weren't so,
Creator would never have allowed us to enter this
world of lessons.

Each of us must remember the beginning of life, the
original agreement as we learned it in the Creation

story of my people. We come from the Stars as a Spiritual energy with one thing in common: we are students of this world. We enter the purest pools of water in our mother's womb and take the first breath of life when we are born on to Mother Earth. We feel our Grandfather's Sun's warmth, and receive nourishment from Mother Earth, our new home away from home. We will be imprinted with other lessons that later in life we will sort through and learn from.

Our ancestors gift this tobacco prayer to each of us to be mindful of your truth and strong in your commitment to your journey here on Mother Earth. Just know that your happiness is a creation on its own, just waiting to be birthed for you to nourish and feed everything around you. Everything is a thought that is manifested through your own will; we are surrounded by lessons waiting to be taught. Our ancestors live within each of us and they stand beside us; we are the foundations of their libraries of knowledge.

Each of us must remember that we all have an important task here on Mother Earth. We all matter; we all play a larger part in the movement of humanity.

So journey forward and know that when hard times come before you, you will have the strength to pick yourself back up and move towards the Light that holds unconditional love.

Today is a good day to begin to walk with lightness and journey into the showers of happiness.

Kookum/Great-grandmother Mary Lyons, just an old Ojibwe woman from the far north.

Photo by Jane Feldman

Grandmothers of the Sacred WE gifting a prayer for climate change in Central Park, New York City, in 2015. Pictured are, from left: Jun Yasuda, Buddhist; Grandmother Eila Paul, Maori; Great-grandmother Mary Lyons, Ojibwe; Grandmother Perci, Hopi; Grandmother Moetu, Maori; Grandmother Devi Tide and her husband Michael, Sufi. I am sending a prayer for change invoking the memories of our ancestors.

Photo by Martina Thalhofer

About the Author

Great-Grandmother Mary Lyons, Ojibwe Elder from Minnesota, is a spiritual advisor, storyteller and wisdom keeper. She travels and teaches internationally, sometimes in collaboration with the Indigenous Grandmothers of the Sacred We, a pan-indigenous group led by Sufi teacher Devi Tide. She is the founder of the Minnesota Coalition on Fetal Alcohol Syndrome, an Indian Child Welfare Act Expert Witness and a Native American Family and Child Advocate.

She was a keynote speaker at the Parliament of World Religions in Utah and at the People's Climate March in New York City in 2014. She is a winner of the Congressional Angels in Adoption Award, nominated by Senator Norm Coleman of Minnesota. She currently serves as a counselor for the women's sobriety group Women of Wellbriety International, which she co-founded.

Grandmother Mary was one of many Native children removed from her home and placed in an institution; she has first-hand experience of the negative effects on children and families of alcohol and drug addiction. After her own recovery, guided by her ancestors, she has dedicated her life to helping others, including fostering and adopting many children with family difficulties, disabilities and fetal alcohol syndrome.

About Green Fire Press

Green Fire Press is an independent publishing company dedicated to supporting authors in producing and distributing high-quality books in fiction or non-fiction, poetry or prose. **Find out more at Greenfirepress.com.**

Other Green Fire Press titles you may also enjoy:

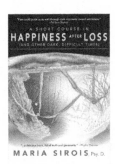

A Short Course In Happiness After Loss, by Maria Sirois, PsyD.

A lyrical gem of a book, combining positive psychology with the wisdom necessary to thrive when facing life's harshest moments, rising through pain into a steady, resilient and open heart.

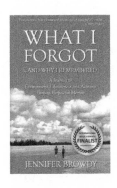

What I Forgot...and Why I Remembered: A Journey to Environmental Awareness and Activism Through Purposeful Memoir, by Jennifer Browdy, PhD.

"Inspires us to see how we can reclaim our lives for the sake of life on Earth" –Joanna Macy.

Finalist for the 2018 International Book Award.

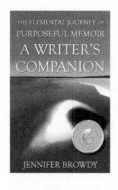

The Elemental Journey of Purposeful Memoir: A Writer's Companion. by Jennifer Browdy, PhD.

Month-by-month guidance for memoir writers.

Winner of the 2017 Nautilus Silver Award.

Writing Fire: Celebrating the Power of Women's Words. Edited by Jennifer Browdy, Jana Laiz and Sahra Bateson Brubeck.

More than 75 passionate women writers share their voices and visions in this powerful anthology.

Nature, Culture & the Sacred: Listening for Women's Leadership. By Nina Simons, co-founder of Bioneers.

Inspiring essays, poetry and interviews with women leaders by one of the foremost environmental justice activists of our time.